The Quilting Sourcebook

The Quilting Sourcebook

Over 200 Easy-to-Follow
Patchwork and Quilting Patterns

Maggi McCormick Gordon

Trafalgar Square Publishing

First published in the United States of America
in 1997 by Trafalgar Square Publishing,
North Pomfret, Vermont 05053

Printed and bound in Italy by Arti Grafiche Garzanti

1 3 5 7 9 8 6 4 2

ISBN 1-57076-096-9

Library of Congress Catalog Card Number
97-60161

Conceived, edited and designed by
Collins & Brown Limited

Editorial Director: Sarah Hoggett
Art Director: Roger Bristow
Editor: Catherine Ward
Designer: Julia Ward-Hastelow
Photographers: Matthew Ward, Sampson Lloyd
Illustrators: Kate Simunek, David Ashby

Reproduction by Bright Arts, Singapore

TECHNIQUES 6

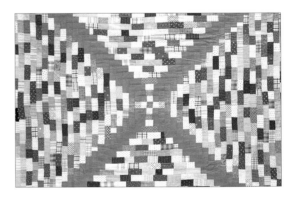

STRIP-PIECING 28

CONTENTS

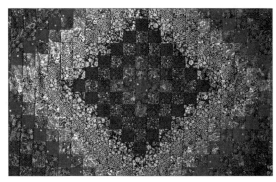

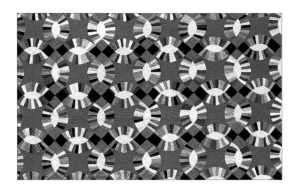

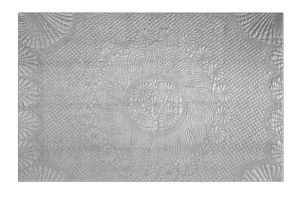

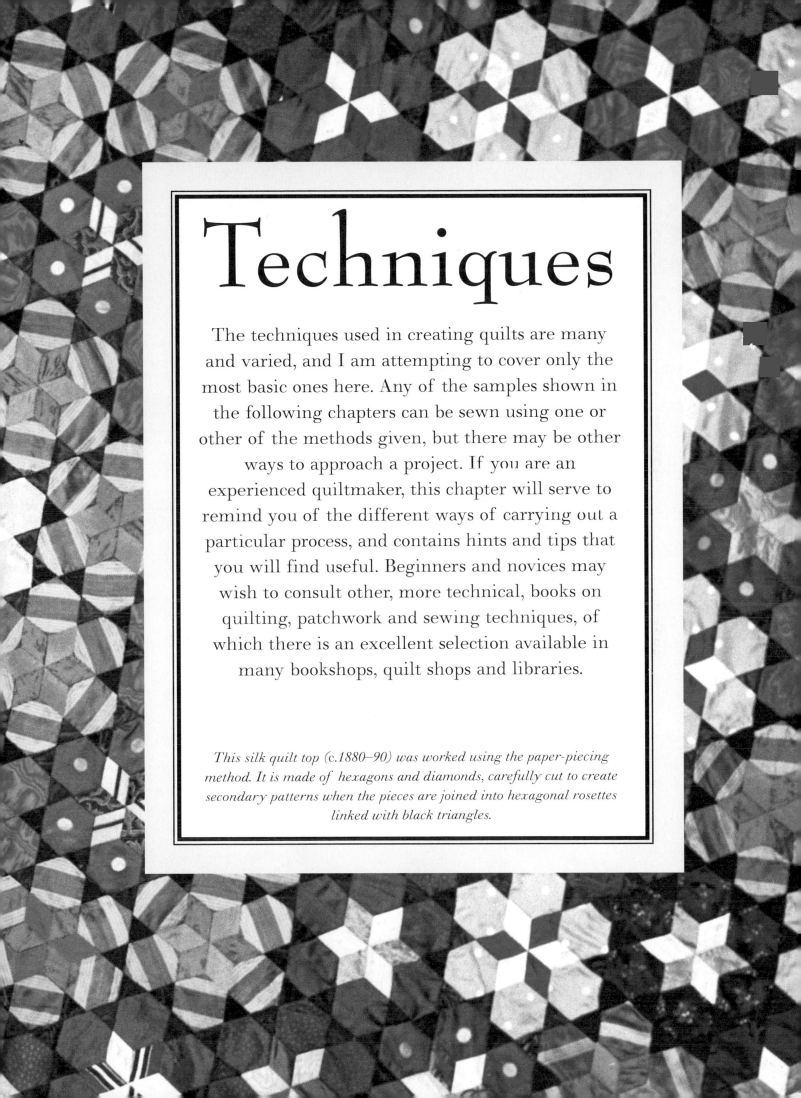

Techniques

The techniques used in creating quilts are many and varied, and I am attempting to cover only the most basic ones here. Any of the samples shown in the following chapters can be sewn using one or other of the methods given, but there may be other ways to approach a project. If you are an experienced quiltmaker, this chapter will serve to remind you of the different ways of carrying out a particular process, and contains hints and tips that you will find useful. Beginners and novices may wish to consult other, more technical, books on quilting, patchwork and sewing techniques, of which there is an excellent selection available in many bookshops, quilt shops and libraries.

This silk quilt top (c.1880–90) was worked using the paper-piecing method. It is made of hexagons and diamonds, carefully cut to create secondary patterns when the pieces are joined into hexagonal rosettes linked with black triangles.

Tools & Equipment

*S*TITCHERS THROUGHOUT THE world have made quilted and patchwork pieces for centuries with little specialist equipment other than scissors, needles and threads. Many of the dressmaker's tools are used by quilters in similar ways, and today there are dozens of specialized pieces of equipment that speed up the labor-intensive processes or make quilting a little easier.

Sewing & Quilting Equipment

The quilter/patchworker needs basic equipment for stitching, including needles, thread, both straight and safety pins and somewhere to keep them safely on hand, and thimbles. Most people embarking on a full-size quilt will use a sewing machine for piecing the top and adding the borders; some will quilt by machine as well.

Threads

For piecing, use ordinary sewing thread to match the fabric: cotton thread for pure cotton, polyester for poly-cotton blends. Silk, linen and wool are used less often for patchwork, but should be stitched with a thread appropriate to their weight and weave. Most people stitch in white or cream, except on particularly dark-colored pieces. Sewing thread can be used for quilting as well, but it needs to be strengthened by waxing (see page 22). Many quilters prefer thread spun especially for quilting, which is heavier and prewaxed. It is available in a reasonable choice of colors. Machine embroidery thread can be used to create special effects.

Sharps

Betweens

Needles

Two types of needles are considered standard for quilters: "sharps", or ordinary sewing needles, for piecing, and "betweens" for quilting. Both come in various sizes, and you will need to experiment to know which size you prefer working with. Dull needles damage fabric and fingers, so be prepared to replace them regularly.

Flat-top thimble

Leather protector

Magnetic thimble

Dressmaker's thimble

Flat-top leather thimble

Thimbles

To thimble or not to thimble? Some people refuse to use them; others swear by them. To execute a quilting stitch without some protection is asking for pricked fingers, however, and the choice is huge. Again, you need to experiment.

Pincushion

Safety pins

Quilter's pins

Pins

Pins are used at several stages in making a patchwork quilt. Ordinary dressmaker's straight pins are needed for holding pieces together during hand piecing, while quilter's safety pins can be used to "baste" the layers of a quilt together for quilting.

Techniques

The techniques used in creating quilts are many and varied, and I am attempting to cover only the most basic ones here. Any of the samples shown in the following chapters can be sewn using one or other of the methods given, but there may be other ways to approach a project. If you are an experienced quiltmaker, this chapter will serve to remind you of the different ways of carrying out a particular process, and contains hints and tips that you will find useful. Beginners and novices may wish to consult other, more technical, books on quilting, patchwork and sewing techniques, of which there is an excellent selection available in many bookshops, quilt shops and libraries.

This silk quilt top (c.1880–90) was worked using the paper-piecing method. It is made of hexagons and diamonds, carefully cut to create secondary patterns when the pieces are joined into hexagonal rosettes linked with black triangles.

Tools & Equipment

*S*TITCHERS THROUGHOUT THE world have made quilted and patchwork pieces for centuries with little specialist equipment other than scissors, needles and threads. Many of the dressmaker's tools are used by quilters in similar ways, and today there are dozens of specialized pieces of equipment that speed up the labor-intensive processes or make quilting a little easier.

Sewing & Quilting Equipment

The quilter/patchworker needs basic equipment for stitching, including needles, thread, both straight and safety pins and somewhere to keep them safely on hand, and thimbles. Most people embarking on a full-size quilt will use a sewing machine for piecing the top and adding the borders; some will quilt by machine as well.

Threads

For piecing, use ordinary sewing thread to match the fabric: cotton thread for pure cotton, polyester for poly-cotton blends. Silk, linen and wool are used less often for patchwork, but should be stitched with a thread appropriate to their weight and weave. Most people stitch in white or cream, except on particularly dark-colored pieces. Sewing thread can be used for quilting as well, but it needs to be strengthened by waxing (see page 22). Many quilters prefer thread spun especially for quilting, which is heavier and prewaxed. It is available in a reasonable choice of colors. Machine embroidery thread can be used to create special effects.

Needles

Two types of needles are considered standard for quilters: "sharps", or ordinary sewing needles, for piecing, and "betweens" for quilting. Both come in various sizes, and you will need to experiment to know which size you prefer working with. Dull needles damage fabric and fingers, so be prepared to replace them regularly.

Sharps

Betweens

Flat-top thimble

Leather protector

Flat-top leather thimble

Magnetic thimble

Dressmaker's thimble

Thimbles

To thimble or not to thimble? Some people refuse to use them; others swear by them. To execute a quilting stitch without some protection is asking for pricked fingers, however, and the choice is huge. Again, you need to experiment.

Pincushion

Quilter's pins

Safety pins

Pins

Pins are used at several stages in making a patchwork quilt. Ordinary dressmaker's straight pins are needed for holding pieces together during hand piecing, while quilter's safety pins can be used to "baste" the layers of a quilt together for quilting.

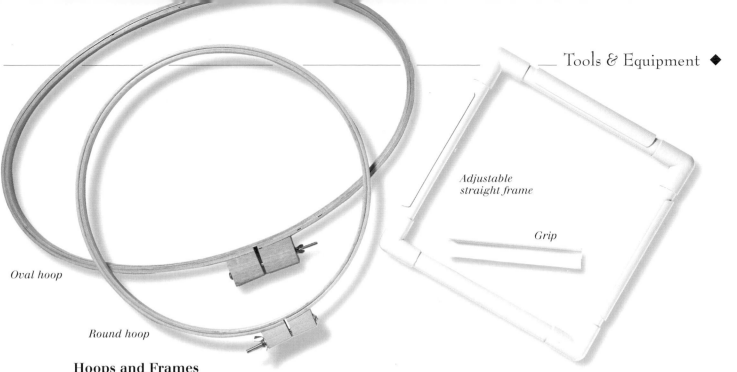

Oval hoop

Round hoop

Adjustable straight frame

Grip

Hoops and Frames

Together with many of the items shown on these two pages, quilting hoops and frames are specialized for their task. Both come in several sizes and shapes, and all are a matter of choice. Most people find it easier to hand quilt accurately if their work is secured in a frame, and the size and shape is determined by the piece being worked.

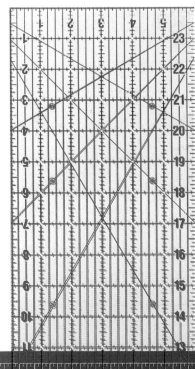

Rotary ruler

Thread scissors

Seam ripper

Paper scissors

Fabric scissors

Cutting Equipment

The rotary cutter, ruler and mat have changed the face of patchwork in the past 20 years, and most of us would be lost without them. They speed up the tedious process of cutting out by giving us unparalleled accuracy and allowing us to cut several layers at once, and the strips that we cut with them can be stitched speedily and chain-pieced (see page 17). But scissors are still essential for cutting curves, templates, trimming and snipping threads. Keep three pairs handy: sharp fabric scissors, paper scissors, which should also be used for cutting batting, and small thread scissors.

Cutting mat

Rotary cutter

Templates and Stencils

Ready-made metal or plastic templates come in an array of styles and sizes, and although they can be expensive, they are also highly accurate and long-lasting. The "window" sets have a solid inner piece with a separate see-through outer piece. Others are multisized, with $^1/_4$ in (5 mm) variations. Quilting stencils are usually made of translucent plastic. If you prefer to make your own templates, there are useful aids for cutting and measuring accurately. The quilter's quarter and quarter-inch wheel are used for adding a $^1/_4$ in (5 mm) seam allowance to straight and curved seams.

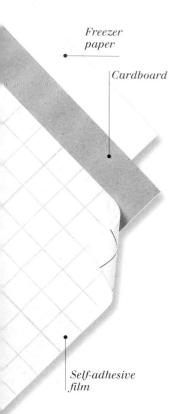

Freezer paper

Cardboard

Self-adhesive film

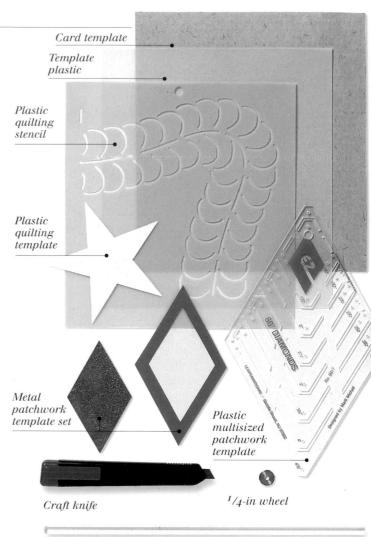

Card template

Template plastic

Plastic quilting stencil

Plastic quilting template

Metal patchwork template set

Plastic multisized patchwork template

Craft knife

$^1/_4$-in wheel

Quilter's quarter

Marking Equipment

Marking tools have become highly specialized in the past few years. Some quilters still prefer ordinary lead pencil used lightly, tailor's chalk or a tailor's pencil. But none of these wash out, and tailor's chalk can be difficult to manipulate. Among the newer options are chalk and soapstone pencils, chalk wheels, and silver quilter's pencils that can be erased from many fabrics. For quilting, I prefer to mark straight lines with $^1/_4$ in (5 mm) masking tape, which can be laid on the fabric and removed after stitching.

Tissue paper

Dressmaker's carbon paper

$^1/_4$ in (5 mm) masking tape

Chalk pencil

Lead pencil

Soapstone pencil

Transfer pencil

Silver quilter's pencil

Fade-away pen

Water-soluble pen

Watercolor pencil

Tailor's pencil

Tailor's chalk

Chalk wheel

Measuring Equipment

Patchwork is about accuracy, and accuracy is about measuring. The measuring tools you need can almost all be found in a sewing box or in a desk; the rest can usually be borrowed from the workshop or a handy student. Compass, protractor and set square are for measuring angles and drawing regular curves. Ruler, tape measure, T-square and seam gauge are for determining distances and drawing straight lines. The flexible curve is an artist's tool for making curves of any size that hold their shape while you reproduce them exactly. Tracing paper is almost essential for patchwork and quilting; squared and isometric graph paper are extremely useful for the accurate drafting of templates.

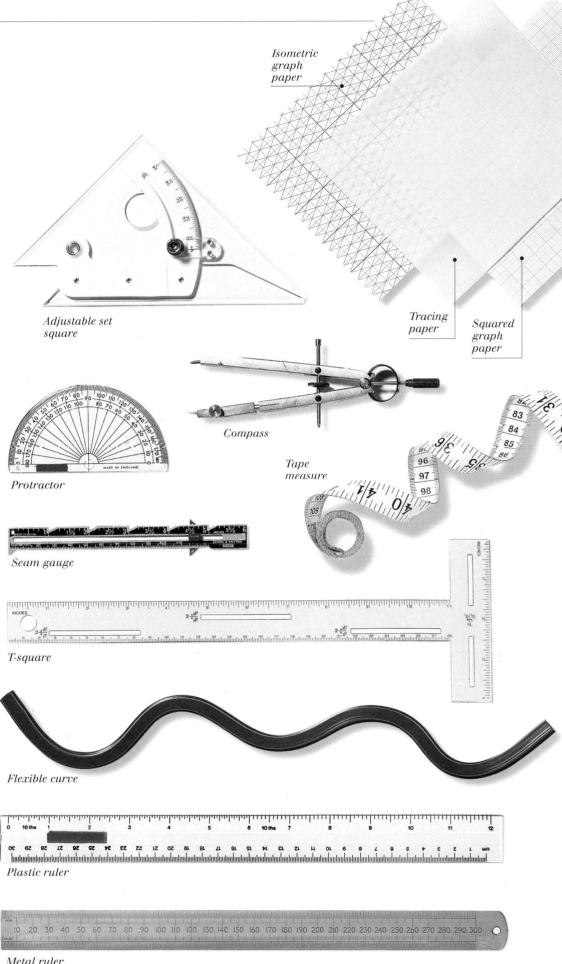

Isometric graph paper

Tracing paper

Squared graph paper

Adjustable set square

Compass

Protractor

Tape measure

Seam gauge

T-square

Flexible curve

Plastic ruler

Metal ruler

Templates, Marking & Cutting

*T*HE FIRST STAGE IN MAKING patchwork is to make the patches. There are two basic methods. making templates so that you can outline the shape to be cut out on the fabric, and rotary cutting. Making templates is a traditional way and is widely used for working with irregular shaped pieces, while the straight edges that can be cut quickly with a rotary cutter are easy to stitch into strips that speed up the assembly process.

Tip: Fabric Grain

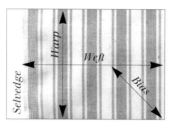

All fabric has three "grains", or directions of woven threads. The lengthwise threads, the "warp", are strung on the loom, with the "weft" threads crossing them horizontally in and out, under and over. The rigid edges on each side of a length of fabric are called "selvedges". The diagonal grain is the "bias". The warp and weft threads remain fairly stationary under tension, but the bias, which has more give and elasticity, stretches more easily and must be handled carefully.

Making Templates

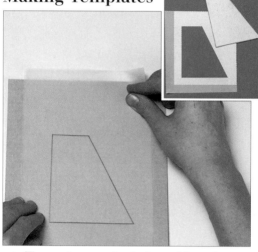

1 Trace the required shape(s) to the correct size and glue the tracing securely to a piece of cardboard. Inset: use a craft knife, and a straightedge if necessary, to cut the shape out precisely.

2 Place the cardboard template on a sheet of template plastic and draw around the shape. To make a window template, add a ¹/4 in (5 mm) seam allowance around all sides of the template – here, we have used a quilter's quarter for accuracy.

3 Using a craft knife and metal ruler, carefully cut out the inner "window" and then the extended template around the outside edge. The inner "window" can be used to mark the stitching line as well as the support papers, if these are used, while the outer section can be used for cutting fabric patches to the correct size.

Marking Fabric and Cutting by Hand

1 *In the "English" method of patchwork (see page 14), fabric is mounted on paper for support. The papers are cut to the finished size, so mark using the inside line of the window template. Cut a paper for each patch.*

2 *Place the window template on the fabric; align the grain if possible. Draw around the template inside and out. Do not drag the marker or you may stretch the fabric. The outer line is the cutting line; the inner line is the stitching line.*

3 *Cut out each fabric patch along the outer line. Pin a paper to the wrong side of each fabric patch and set them aside until you are ready to stitch. When you cut fabric, always use sharp dressmaker's scissors to minimize stretching and the tendency to fray.*

Rotary Cutting

Tip: Cutting Stitched Strips

Speed is the principle behind strip-piecing (see pages 28–49). Rotary-cut strips are stitched together along their length in a particular order and then cut into short lengths to create a number of identical pre-pieced units. After stitching, press the seams to one side. Lay the pieced strip on the cutting mat, align the ruler across it and cut into strips of the desired width.

1 *Rotary cutting is a method based on 20th-century technology and the modern liking for speed in all things. Fold the washed and pressed fabric along the straight grain to fit on the cutting mat. Level off the edge to be cut. Place the ruler over the "good" fabric to avoid cutting into it, and hold it steady while you trim away the uneven edge. Always cut away from yourself.*

2 *Turn the fabric so that the ruler covers the area that you want to end up with. Use either the marked ruler or mat – never both – to measure, then cut strips of the desired width along the grain, usually from selvedge to selvedge.*

    There are many different versions of mats, rulers and cutters available – if possible, experiment with them in classes or workshops before you buy.

Hand Piecing

*W*HILE MANY PATTERNS lend themselves to the ease and security of machine stitching, others are easier and more accurately worked by hand. There are a few traditional designs, especially among the curved patterns, which are difficult to stitch on the machine and are almost always hand sewn. The technique known as English patchwork involves basting fabric shapes to paper to achieve the correct shape, and joining them by hand.

Hand Stitches

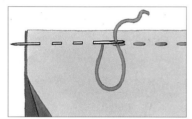

Running Stitch
Take the needle in and out of the fabric several times, picking up small, evenly spaced stitches. Pull the needle gently through the fabric until the thread is taut, then repeat the sequence to continue stitching.

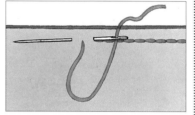

Backstitch
Bring the needle through to the right side, then insert it back a short distance behind where it first came out. Bring the point out ahead of the resulting stitch the same distance in front of the needle, and repeat the sequence to continue.

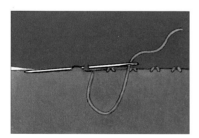

Slipstitch
Hide the knot in one folded edge and pull the needle and thread through. Pick up a thread or two in the opposite edge and insert the needle back in the first side, next to where the first thread came out. Slide the needle along for a short distance inside the fold, and repeat.

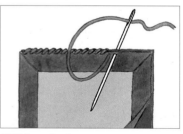

Whipstitch
Also called overcasting or oversewing, this stitch is worked from left to right. Insert the needle at a slight angle from back to front, picking up one or two threads on each side of the folded edge in each stitch. Pull the thread until it is gently taut, and repeat.

English Patchwork

1 *Pin a backing paper to the wrong side of a fabric patch, matching the edges of the paper to the marked stitching line. Fold the seam allowance over the paper and baste in place, knotting the thread on the right side.*

2 *Hold two patches right sides together and make sure the corners are level. Whipstitch the edges together (see left), taking care not to catch the backing papers – these are removed after all the blocks have been joined together.*

Setting In

English patchwork is especially useful for setting in patches with sharp angles. To join three diamonds to make this block, match the inside point of the third piece and, working from the center out, whipstitch one side, then the other. The insets show the finished block from the right side (left) and wrong side (right).

Straight Seams

1 With right sides together, pin the patches along the straight seam, matching the corners on each piece. We have added a pin in the center – you may need more, depending on the length of the seam.

2 Use running stitch or backstitch to sew along the marked seam. Be sure to begin and end precisely at the corners, and stitch only on the marked line. Handle bias seams with care to prevent stretching.

Four-piece Seams

1 Stitching over seams can be tricky when you sew by hand. Here, two squares are joined along the marked stitching line, then two more squares are added, making two units of two squares each.

2 To join the two units into a four-patch block, press the seams in opposite directions. Place the units right sides together and push a pin through from back to front, marking the center seams precisely. Pin the seam as usual.

3 Working from the center out, use running stitch or backstitch to join the two units first on one side, then the other. Finish precisely at the outside corners on each side, taking care not to stitch into the seam allowance.

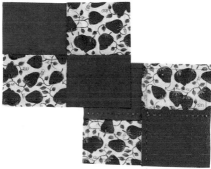

Seen from the right side (top), the units have been turned into a block in which the corners meet exactly in the middle. The wrong side (bottom) shows the precision needed at each corner of the marked square.

Pressing Seams

Fingerpressing

Unlike seams in dressmaking, those used to join patch-work pieces can be less thoroughly pressed at the early stages, especially when you are work-

ing with small pieces. Simply press the seam down on the wrong side with a finger or thumb to make it lie flat, but be careful not to pull hard enough to stretch the fabric.

Pressing with an Iron

Seams are usually pressed to one side (although there are exceptions). "Press" means just that – do not drag the iron along the

seam or you may stretch it. With the iron set at the appropriate temperature, simply press down on the wrong side long enough to make the seam lie flat in the chosen direction.

Machine Piecing

*Q*UILTMAKERS HAVE USED sewing machines since early home models were introduced in the 1830s and 1840s. Hand-turned and treadle machines are still used by Amish quilters and are widespread in Third World countries, while electric versions have been computerized to carry out a wide variety of sewing tasks. Patchworkers have refined machine techniques in recent years to speed up the piecing process, creating a new science from an old art.

Tip: Marking a 1/4 in (5 mm) Seam

Most machines can be fitted with a special foot that measures a precise 1/4 in (5 mm) seam, but you can mark the needle plate with a piece of masking tape along which to guide the seam. Make sure the ends are stuck down securely, and replace grubby strips regularly. Test the width of the seam allowance on a scrap of fabric each time you put on a new length of tape.

Stitching Strips

1 Place two strips right sides together and line up the edges to be joined. There is no need to pin or mark stitching lines, but sewing straight seams may require practice.

2 Taking a standard 1/4 in (5 mm) seam allowance, sew a straight seam down the entire length of the strips, keeping the edges level.

Joining Pieced Units

1 To combine pieced units, align the edges to be joined, right sides together. If seams on the pieced strips are pressed to one side, they should fit together neatly, one in each direction.

2 The joined unit, shown here from both the front and back, has evenly matched rows with squared-up corners at each meeting point.

Stitching Curves

1 First mark the sewing line on the wrong sides. Placing pins at right angles to the curved edge, pin the patches right sides together, first in the center, then at each end, then in between.

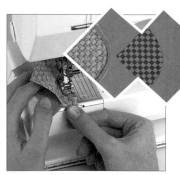

2 Insert the needle at one edge and follow the marked stitching line, removing pins as you work. Finish at the other edge and press toward the concave curve.

Chain-piecing

1 *Place piles of units to be joined within easy reach and feed them through the machine one after the other, without lifting the presser foot or breaking the thread.*

2 *The chain of units, held together by short threads, is cut apart once they have all been pieced. If this method is repeated at each stage in making a block, the piecing process is speeded up.*

Joining Pieced and Plain Blocks

1 *Many patterns involve joining a plain block, such as a square, to a pieced unit. The pieced unit, such as the triangle patch here, is made first, taking a standard $^{1}/_{4}$ in (5 mm) seam allowance.*

2 *When a plain square is joined to a triangle unit, the top corner is caught in the seam, and the distance between the edge of the block and the visible corner of the triangle is $^{1}/_{4}$ in (5 mm).*

3 *If two units are combined to make a four-patch block, the seam allowances become hidden and the four corners meet precisely in the middle.*

Unpicking

Sometimes you may need to unpick a stitched seam, either because you made a mistake or because the construction method involves sewing a series of seams that are then manipulated before one or more of them are opened up again.

Ripping a Closed Seam

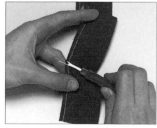 

1 Holding the seam taut, insert the point of the seam ripper into a stitch near the end of the stitching and break the thread. Repeat every third or fourth stitch.

2 Lift the end of one layer of stitched fabric and, holding the lower layer flat, pull the top layer gently to separate the stitches.

Ripping an Open Seam

Holding the seam open with right sides facing you, insert the ripper between the layers and break the thread. Pull the seam apart gently and repeat.

Tip: Tension

Achieving a smooth line of stitching is crucial to successful patchwork and quilting. To make a perfect stitch, thread tension must be balanced top and bottom. Always test the tension on a representative sample of work before you begin to stitch.

Balanced stitch
The two threads join in the middle of the layers of fabric and look identical on both sides.

Bottom thread too tight
The bobbin tension is too tight if the lower thread lies in a line and the top thread shows through onto the back of the seam. Loosen the bobbin thread according to the instructions in the machine manual.

Top thread too tight
The needle thread is too tight if the upper thread lies in a line and the lower thread is visible on the top of the seam. Loosen the thread in the needle according to the instructions in the machine manual.

Sashing & Borders

*W*HEN ALL THE BLOCKS FOR a quilt are completed, they must be joined and a border added to finish off the edges. Some blocks are joined edge to edge, thereby creating secondary patterns, while others need to be separated by narrow strips of fabric called sashing to set them apart. Borders, usually a narrow inner one combined with a wider outer one, enclose the design and hold the quilt together visually.

Tip: Deciding Border Size

The width of the border depends of course on the quilt: its overall size, the size and complexity of the blocks, whether it is an inner or an outer border. Inner borders can provide a frame, especially on a complex pattern, that sets off the design. They should usually be no more than 1¹/2 in (3.5 cm) wide finished. Outer borders or single ones are wider, up to 4 in (10 cm) finished in some cases. Remember to add seam allowances on each side of the strip when cutting out.

Sashing

 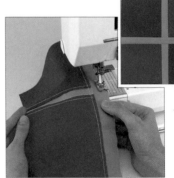

1 *Sashing usually runs both horizontally and vertically. Cut sashing strips, ideally a little longer than the block to be sashed, to the desired width plus seams.*

2 *Join a short strip to one side of the block, then join the next block to the other side of the strip. Repeat to make rows of sashed blocks as required.*

3 *Stitch a long strip to one row of sashed blocks, then join the next row to the other long edge of the strip. The inset shows four blocks that have been sashed together.*

Straight Borders

Top and Tail
Straight borders are added to the top and bottom – short – edges first. A side border is then applied to each long edge.

Round and Round
This method is a little less straightforward, but is attractive and can make better use of fabric. Start on any edge 3–4 in (7.5–10 cm) down from the top corner and apply the first strip, which must overhang the top edge of the quilt by at least  *the width of the border strip. Add the second, third and fourth strips, working in a clockwise direction. Finish by opening out the first strip and continuing the line of stitching, catching in the end of the fourth strip. Square off the corners if necessary.*

Corners

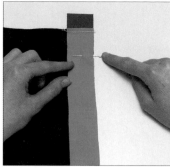

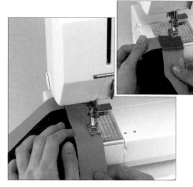

1 Corner squares can be incorporated into borders and sashing. Cut strips for the border and contrasting squares the same width for the corners. Stitch a square to one end of each strip – these have been chain-pieced. Press the seams to one side.

2 Line up the first strip so that the corner overhangs the top edge of the piece being bound or sashed. Mark the beginning of the seam about 3–4 in (7.5–10 cm) below the top of the quilt with a pin, and start stitching here.

3 Working around the sides of the quilt in a clockwise direction, add the remaining strips. Inset: When you get back to the beginning, incorporate the first corner square, continuing the initial seam.

Here, the bordered piece is shown from both sides. On the right side, the corners meet precisely. On the wrong side, note that the seams are pressed in the direction required by the construction.

Mitered Corners

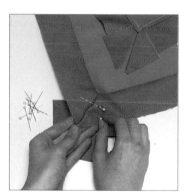

1 Mitered corners must be neat and precise. Cut strips longer than the width of the quilt plus borders. Measure a point $1/4$ in (5 mm) in from the corner of the quilt and apply a strip in each direction, starting at the marked point.

2 Fold back each strip to a 45-degree angle and press to mark the fold (top). Working from the right side, pin along the fold to hold the seam in place.

3 Turn the corner to the wrong side and re-pin with the pins at right angles to the fold (top). Make sure the two foldlines match precisely on both sides and stitch from the inner corner toward the edge. Trim the ends.

The miter is smooth and even, giving a professional finish to the edge of the quilt.

Pieced Borders

Making a border from leftover pieces of the quilt fabric requires more work than applying a straight one, but it can repay the extra effort handsomely. A well-executed pieced border gives a quilt pizzazz and flair like nothing else can.

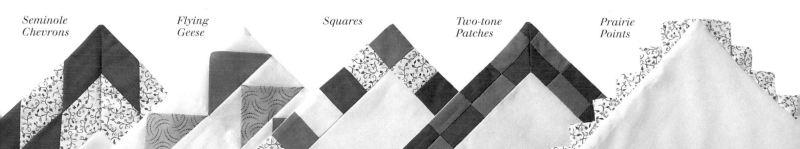

Seminole Chevrons   Flying Geese   Squares   Two-tone Patches   Prairie Points

The Four Bs

THE FOUR Bs OF QUILTING — batting, backing, bagging and basting — are stages between finishing the quilt top and beginning the quilting. Batting is both the material of the middle layer and the process of padding the quilt. Backing is the fabric used on the back of the quilt, as well as its application. Bagging is a way of backing and finishing the edges in the same operation. Basting is the stitching that holds the layers in place while you quilt.

Batting

80% polyester, 20% cotton

Polyester needlepunch

Cotton

Dark gray polyester

2oz (60g) polyester

4oz (125g) polyester

Batting, or wadding, is the padded material used in the middle of a quilt to provide warmth and softness. Originally made of old rough blankets, extra layers of fabric, or combed wool or cotton fibers, its modern equivalent is available cut to size or in rolls that can be measured like fabric. Synthetic polyester is the most widely used, with cotton and cotton/polyester blends also popular. Wool and silk versions are available, usually only by special order. Batting normally comes in white, but a dark gray version can also be found.

Backing

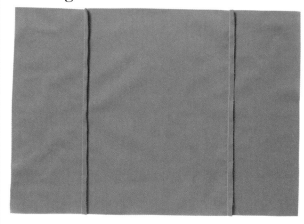

Backing fabric should match or coordinate with the quilt top, and should be of a weight and weave that are easy to quilt. To avoid having a seam in the center of an extra-wide quilt, place a full width in the center and add a narrower panel on each side, as shown.

Turning a Corner

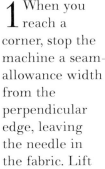

1 When you reach a corner, stop the machine a seam-allowance width from the perpendicular edge, leaving the needle in the fabric. Lift the presser foot and carefully turn the work at a right angle to the seam that you have just stitched.

2 With the needle still in the fabric, lower the presser foot again and continue stitching along the next seamline. This method is the same for all machine sewing.

Bagging

1 *Lay the batting flat on a large table or clean floor and place the quilt top, right side up, on it. Allow some extra batting around all four sides. Place the backing fabric right side down on top and smooth all layers to eliminate wrinkles. Pin around the edges to secure them.*

2 *Stitch all around the edges, taking a seam of $^{1}/_{4} - {^{1}}/_{2}$ in (5–10 mm) along the outer edge of the quilt top and leaving a 5–10 in (12–25 mm) gap in the center of the bottom edge. Cut away the excess batting and backing fabric, trim the corners and turn the quilt right side out through the unstitched gap.*

3 *Turn the raw edges of the gap to the inside and press them gently. Pin and slipstitch the gap closed to finish bagging (see page 14).*

Basting

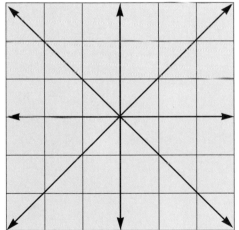

Basting, or tacking, is used to hold the quilt layers together. Bagged quilts cannot be basted until after they have been bagged, but quilts to be bound after the quilting has been completed are basted before quilting, to keep them as smooth as possible. Above: Basting is done vertically and horizontally, and sometimes diagonally, from the center out, with rows about 4 in (10 cm) apart, whether it is stitched or done with safety pins.

1 *Lay the backing fabric right side down on a large flat surface and place the batting on top. Center the batting on the backing and smooth both layers carefully. Lay the quilt top right side up over the batting and smooth it, working from the center to the edges. Use safety pins to hold the three layers together.*

2 *Take large, but not gigantic, slanted or running stitches through all layers, starting in the center and working outward. Keep the layers flat while you work – using the end of the bowl of a spoon to lift the point of the needle as it emerges takes a little practice, but is an effective way to protect fingers.*

Hand Quilting

*Q*UILTING BY HAND HAS BEEN practiced for thousands of years in some form in almost every culture known to historians and anthropologists. What probably began as a way to hold layers of clothing together for warmth became a decorative art that has been handed down from many different places. By the 16th and 17th centuries, European seamstresses were using quilting to embellish clothing and soft furnishings in a tradition that continues today.

Tip: Strengthening Thread

The act of quilting is hard on thread, which will be pulled numerous times through several layers, including the thick coarse batting. Special quilting thread is heavier and stronger than ordinary sewing thread, but it is available in only a limited choice of colors. Ordinary cotton or cotton/polyester thread can be strengthened by sliding it through a block of beewax before stitching.

Marking Straight Lines

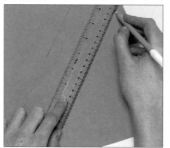

Using a Ruler
Quilting patterns should be transferred onto the finished quilt top before the piece is assembled and basted. Straight lines can be drawn on the piece using a ruler and a suitable marker.

Using Masking Tape
Straight lines can also be delineated using 1/4 in (5 mm) masking tape, applied onto the surface after the piece has been basted. Take care not to stretch the tape.

Transferring with Tissue Paper

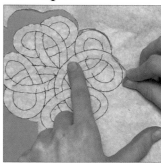

1 Some intricate designs, especially for corded quilting (see page 25), are best transferred by basting a tissue-paper tracing of the pattern onto the fabric, using small basting stitches and contrasting thread.

2 When all lines have been stitched, run the point of a pin or needle gently around the drawn lines. This will tear the paper along the stitching line so that the outside part of the tissue paper pattern can be removed.

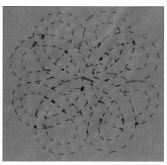

3 Repeat Step 2, working along all the lines of stitching to remove all the pieces of the paper pattern. Always pull gently so you don't loosen the stitches.

4 With the paper removed, the lines of the pattern can be seen clearly. It is easier to remove the basting threads after quilting if you knot them on the right side.

Making and Using Templates

1 The quilting patterns in this book can be enlarged or reduced on a photocopier and then traced onto the template plastic or cardboard.

2 This template was drawn directly onto template plastic and cut out carefully, then laid on the fabric. The stitching line is marked in pencil.

3 Chalk is used to mark the design on the dark part of the quilt. All marks should be as light as possible.

Ways to Quilt

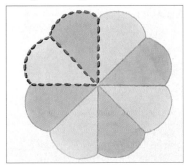

In the Ditch
Follow the seamlines of the pieced pattern to secure the layers and give texture to the top. This method does not need to be marked.

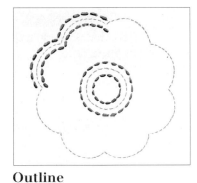

Outline
Follow the seamlines of the pieced pattern or the edges of an appliqué motif, positioning the stitching 1/4 in (5 mm) to the side of the motif. Marking is useful but not essential.

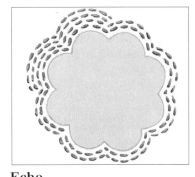

Echo
Repeat the outline around a motif at intervals so the shape of the motif fills the background area around it. Again, marking will help keep the distance between the lines of stitching equidistant.

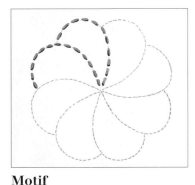

Motif
To quilt a motif or a medallion, mark the shape on the fabric and stitch around the outline. Make the marks as faint as possible, but make sure you are still able to see them.

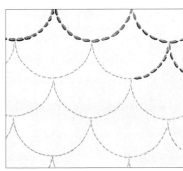

Filling Patterns
All-over patterns can be used to fill in background areas with dense stitching, or to make a grid or create a secondary pattern with quilting that is not directly related to the motif.

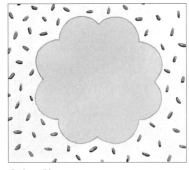

Stippling
Stipple quilting produces dense areas of random stitching that flatten the texture or soften the effect.

Quilting Stitch

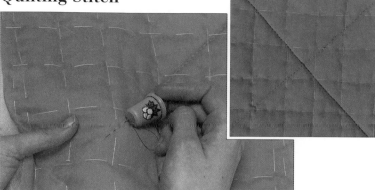
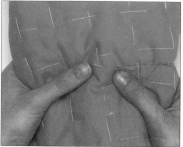

This is not an ordinary running stitch, and it requires practice. Insert the needle through all layers and tilt it up, again piercing all layers. Repeat to take two or three more even stitches, then pull the thread through to the end. Entire books have been written on this subject, and I found it easier to understand by having someone demonstrate it to me.

Knots

Knots secure the thread inside the batting layer. Pull the thread through the backing so the knot passes through it, but not through the top layer, and catches in the batting.

Knotting Thread

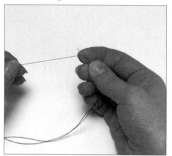

1 Hold the needle between thumb and index finger, with the point upward. Loop the end of the thread around the needle twice, holding it tightly in place.

2 With the loop securely held, pull it down the entire length of thread to the end, where the knot will catch.

Quick Knotting

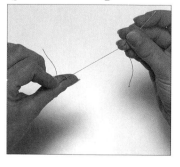

Hold the needle in your sewing hand so the thread cannot slip out. Loop the loose end of thread around the first finger of the other hand and, holding it securely, roll the loop off the finger into a knot.

Travelling

1 *To move the needle a distance of several inches without taking a stitch, you can "travel" through the batting. Bring the point of the needle — and only the point — through to the top.*

2 *Turn the needle over inside the batting so that the threaded eye points roughly in the direction you want to go. Push the eye out through the top about a third of the length of the needle.*

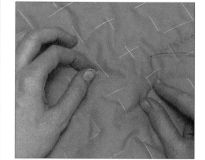

3 *Holding the eye carefully, turn the needle again and bring the point through at the start of the stitching line. Pull the needle and thread all the way out, and begin stitching again.*

Types of Quilting

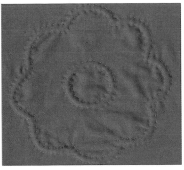  

Corded (Front and Back)

This elegant version of quilting, also known as Italian quilting, was widely used in the 17th and 18th centuries, and enjoyed a revival in the 1920s. It is suitable for curved and flowing lines, but not for sharp angles. The fabric is backed with cheesecloth (muslin) onto which the pattern has been transferred. A channel is stitched in running stitch or backstitch, and a cord is inserted into the channel.

Sashiko

This Japanese technique, used to hold several layers of fabric together for worker's clothing, uses thicker thread and larger stitches. It is traditionally worked white on blue or red fabric.

  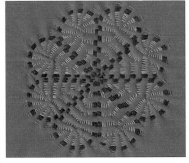

Trapunto (Front and Back)

This padded method of quilting provides interesting texture and a background for embellishment with beads, embroidery, and so on. The fabric is marked with the design and backed with a thinner fabric. Both layers are stitched with running stitch or backstitch. Slits are made in the backing and stuffed lightly, then sewn back together with herringbone stitches.

Kantha

This heavily stitched technique from Bangladesh also originated as a utility method of securing thin layers of fabric, usually worn saris, together.

Utility Quilting

Also known as big-stitch quilting, the stitches used here are based on embroidery stitches, and can be worked in embroidery threads or even ribbons. They have a rough-and-ready look that works well with many traditional patchwork patterns, and have the advantage of being quick to stitch.

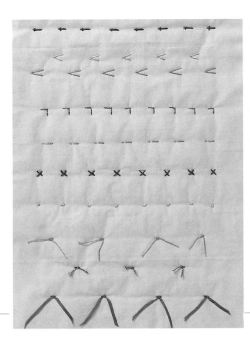

Mennonite Tack

Crow's Foot

Half-buttonhole

Methodist Knot

Cross Stitch

French Knot

Running Tie

Decorative Tie

Ribbon Tie

Machine Quilting & Binding

*Q*UILTING BY MACHINE was traditionally the ugly stepsister of the art, but the advent of sewing machines designed to cope with the layers — and especially the speed possible — have brought the skill into its own in recent years. Well-worked machine quilting is attractive and versatile, aided by the range of machine-embroidery threads. Always test a sample piece first and adjust the tension accordingly. Binding the edges is the final stage of making a quilt.

Straight Lines

Straight lines can be marked on the fabric and stitched, or simply mark one line and then use the foot as a guide. A special walking foot helps keep the layers travelling at the same speed.

Curved Lines

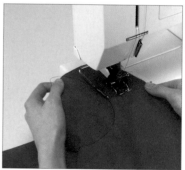

Curved lines can be marked on the fabric beforehand and stitched, or the curve can be followed using a special bar that measures the distance from one line to the next as you work.

Meander Stitch

The machine version of stippling, this stitch gives a lovely close stitched texture as it winds its random way through the area to be quilted. This method works best if lines are not overstitched.

Quilt-as-you-go

1 *Cut out strips of fabric of the desired width and cut a piece of batting about 2 in (5 cm) bigger all around than*

the desired finished size of the piece. Lay two strips right sides together and place them wrong side down on the edge of the batting. Stitch along the right-hand edge of the strips through all the layers, then fold back the top strip.

2 *Place a third strip right side down over the second strip and stitch in place. Repeat the process to cover the batting.*

Rolling

A large quilt can be difficult to handle under the machine. Roll up the edges to the area being stitched, to distribute the weight and make it easier to move the piece around. Bicycle clips can be used to hold the roll in place.

Single Binding

1 Mark a point in each corner ¹/₄ in (5 mm) in from each side edge. Press a ¹/₄ in (5 mm) seamline on one long edge of the binding strips, which should be cut on the straight grain.

2 Pin the binding in position at the corner, right side of top to right side of binding strip, along the unpressed edge. Stitch in place, starting and finishing at a marked point.

Double Binding

1 Double binding is stronger than single binding, and is useful for quilts to be laundered frequently. Cut strips twice as wide as the finished binding plus ¹/₂ in (10 mm) seam allowances. Fold in half lengthways and press.

Single binding

Double binding

3 Open out the binding and pin a new strip in place along the adjacent edge. Stitch in place between the marked points, taking care not to catch the first strip in the stitching line. Add the remaining strips.

4 Turn the binding to the back and cover all the raw edges. At each corner, fold the end of the strip to the inside and square off the corner. To finish, pin and slipstitch (see page 14) around all edges.

2 Mark, pin and stitch as single binding, sewing along the doubled raw edges of the binding. Turn the folded edge to the back and slipstitch in place to finish.

Edges to Middle

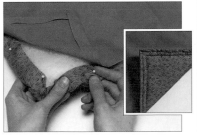

Here, the backing is folded over the edge of the batting and the top edges are folded to the inside. Pin and stitch ¹/₄ in (5 mm) from the edge all around, then stitch ¹/₄ in (5 mm) in from that.

Back to Front

1 Center the top and batting on the backing fabric and trim the edges level. Turn under ¹/₄ in (5 mm) all around the backing. Fold a miter and trim at each corner.

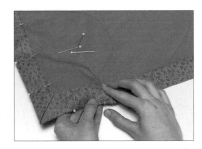

2 Fold the pressed edges of the backing over to the front of the quilt and pin, then stitch in place neatly by hand or machine along all four sides.

This method gives a strong edge and cohesive feel to the quilt.

Strip-piecing

Strip-piecing is perhaps the easiest of all the methods of assembling a quilt top. However, the patterns that can be created are among the most interesting and exciting. From the random vivacity of a string-pieced work to the formality of Log Cabin or Irish Chain, strip-piecing consists of cutting strips of a specific width and reassembling them into the chosen pattern.

The method of strip-piecing can also be used to make sashing and borders, and some of the patterns found in other chapters can be put together using elements of strip-piecing techniques.

This fascinating variation of Bricks or Steps (c.1920) could be assembled by piecing strips of different lengths using random fabrics.

Quilt Gallery

TRIP-PIECING provides a way of using up leftover scraps of fabric and of making an item of a particular size or shape. The method has probably been used since the beginning of stitching to join pieces of cloth and leather. Traditional strip-piecing features in a number of quilting traditions, from the frugal Amish to the impoverished African-American, and was widely used by 18th- and 19th-century quilters on the American frontier where new fabric was notoriously hard to obtain.

Joining long pieces of fabric with straight seams by hand is, of course, a tedious process, but with the advent of the sewing machine in the mid-19th century, strip-piecing became a time-saving way to assemble a quilt more quickly and more accurately.

However, the modern method of strip-piecing has evolved in the past 20 or 30 years, with the invention of the rotary cutter and its attendant accessories, the rotary ruler and the self-healing cutting mat. The pieces for a quilt top can now be cut in a matter of minutes instead of hours or even days, and the strips can be joined accurately by machine into complex patterns involving simple straight-sided shapes or precise angles.

Today, quilters and designers are continually coming up with new ways to use the labor-saving devices on hand to create easier-to-assemble variations on traditional designs, as well as some new patterns of their own.

Log Cabin and Beyond

The pattern used perhaps most often to teach beginners the rudiments of strip-piecing is Log Cabin, an old favorite that

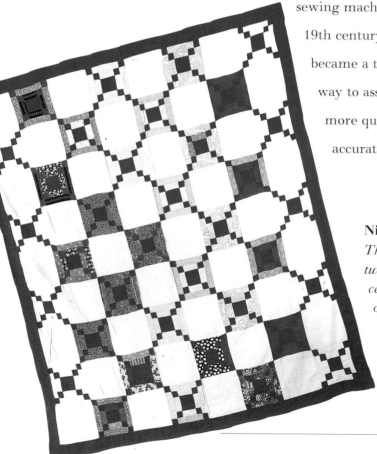

Nine-patch Chain
This bedcover, made mainly from cotton twill, dates from the second half of the 19th century. The main colors are Turkey red, one of the most widely used colors of the period, and white — although some of the blocks combine other printed fabrics, including florals, paisleys and oriental motifs. The result is a diagonal chain that runs through the entire quilt.

Straight Furrow Log Cabin

The bright colors and large-scale blocks make this late 19th-century double-bed quilt somewhat out of the ordinary. The use of alternating red strips between the yellow on the light side and the black on the dark side is another unusual feature. Traditionally, the center of a Log Cabin block is red, representing the hearth fire at the center of the cabin. Here, it is made from a red-and-yellow print that blends into the yellow strips on one side, while being sharply delinated from the black strips on the other.

was originally worked by hand, often mounted on a block of muslin (calico). The design, which has many variations, first appeared in the 1850s and '60s, leading some historians to relate it to President Abraham Lincoln, the most famous resident of a log cabin. It was beloved by Victorian seamstresses on both sides of the Atlantic, who made numerous examples in silk and velvet and some in wool, and is still popular today, although it is more often made in cotton. However, being easy to cut and to stitch does not make Log Cabin boring. The variations

such as Courthouse Steps, Chevron Logs, Off-center Logs and Pineapple, as well as the different ways of setting the blocks together, make the possibilities of this pattern endless.

Another simple strip pattern, Rail Fence, which shares Log Cabin's pioneer background and probably has as many variations, is more limited in its setting possibilities but can be used to create beautifully simple pieces.

Bricks and Steps are both variations of string-piecing, which provide a good way of using up narrow lengths of leftover

African-American String-pieced Quilt

This beautifully primitive string-pieced quilt, made c.1935, is representative of its tradition in its bold use of random color, its disregard for strict geometric rules, and its use of whatever pieces were on hand regardless of size and shape. Its African roots – Ghanian weaving, in particular – are clear, and its liveliness makes it a highly desirable piece of work.

fabric and long scraps. Several modern quilters have made this technique their own, creating interesting pictorial and landscape works using "strings" of varying widths, in an updated version of a method which was widely used by slave quilters before the American Civil War.

Roman stripe is another strip-pieced pattern, which looks wonderful worked in traditional "Amish" colors. Popular with Amish quiltmakers since the end of the 19th century, it consists of one right-angled triangle pieced in multicolored strips, usually of an even width, combined with another right-angled triangle in a plain, solid color, usually black or dark blue. This creates a contrast that makes the colors

shimmer and almost twinkle. Most versions are set square so that the strips run diagonally across the quilt, but examples exist in which blocks are turned on point, giving a very different feel to the pattern.

THE NINE-PATCH

One of the most versatile of all patchwork patterns is the nine-patch. It can be as simple as nine squares arranged three by three in a checked fashion, or as mind-bogglingly complex as a series of geometric combinations of smaller squares or triangles. Nine-patch patterns occur

Brick Steps

The diagonal line in art and design gives movement and life, a principle illustrated extremely well by this pattern, which might also be called Streak of Lightning. Made c.1875 from only two fabrics, a plain red and a red-and-white print, this quilt is enhanced and contained by the sawtooth border.

throughout the history of quiltmaking, and appear in Amish Bars quilts, as corners in borders and sashing, and turned on point. Each patch can be made of more complicated patterns such as a double nine-patch, made of five nine-patch squares combined with four plain ones. Another popular pattern is the "chain" in Single Irish Chain, which is formed from setting nine-patch blocks with large plain square blocks. Hand-sewn at first, today's strip-piecing techniques allow us to create strikingly beautiful machine-stitched versions of nine-patch that are quick to cut out and assemble.

SEMINOLE PATTERNS

Seminole patterns are doubly strip-pieced, since not only are they assembled by the strip-piecing method, but the piece created is invariably a strip of pieced fabric. Created by stitching strips and then cutting these into pieces that are stitched again, usually at a sharp angle, Seminole is a true 20th-century innovation. In the early 1900s, sewing machines became available to members of the Seminole tribe, and women began to decorate their clothes with traditional designs made in a new way. They were soon producing items displaying the diagonal patterns on a commercial scale – skirts, blouses, jackets and bags in bright

Double Irish Chain
Made c.1845–55, this beautiful version of Double Irish Chain uses two shades of brown for the chain set against white, which extends into the unusual border of flowers made from blue and beige prints. Irish Chain is an old pattern that would certainly have been well known at the time this quilt was made.

colors are among the products that are still made and sold to a wide market.

The patterns shown in this chapter are only a few of the designs that can be strip-pieced, but they should provide you with ideas for creating your own heirloom or masterpiece, quickly and accurately.

Nine-patch Patterns

Nine-patch

The basic nine-patch block is one of the simplest of all quilt blocks, and at the same time one of the most versatile. It can be made from individual squares, or strip-pieced using two different arrangements. The top and bottom rows can be cut from the same pieced strip, while the middle row is cut from three strips of fabric arranged in the opposite order. The variations shown opposite represent only some of the nine-patch possibilities, and a number of the blocks shown throughout the book are based on this form.

How to Construct a Nine-patch Block

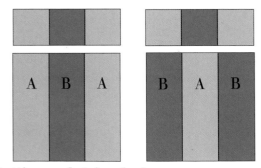

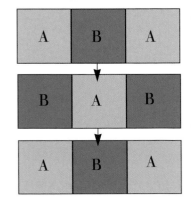

Joining rows

Matching the seams, stitch three of the pieced rows together into a block, alternating between ABA and BAB settings.

Cutting and strip-piecing

Cut the fabrics into strips one-third as wide as the finished block plus seam allowances, and arrange in alternating sequence, ABA and BAB. Taking a $1/4$ in (5 mm) seam, stitch the strips together along their long edges. Cut across the pieced strips in rows one-third as wide as the finished block plus seam allowances.

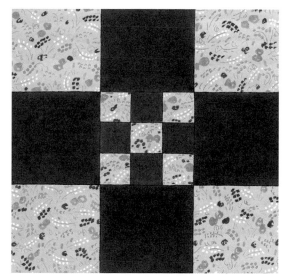

Double Nine-patch I

At the center of this version of double nine-patch is a smaller nine-patch that gives the finished block the look of a cross with its reflection in the middle. The center could also be made of different fabrics from the surrounding larger squares.

Double Nine-patch II

This double nine-patch block consists of five identical small nine-patch units pieced to four large plain squares. If several of these blocks are joined together into a larger piece, the chain effect created by the small squares that run diagonally from opposite corners is greatly emphasized and enhanced. In fact, this block is made in the same way as the pieced block used in Irish Chain (see page 48).

Chain and Hourglass

This fascinating pattern is aptly named. Viewed horizontally, it creates distinct links of a chain that alternate from one set to the next. Look at it vertically, and you will see the hourglass shapes. It could be made more complex – and more complicated to construct – by using two different fabrics in addition to the background, shown here as dark, to make the shapes even clearer.

Rail Fence Patterns

Rail Fence

The simplest form of Rail Fence consists of three fabrics, which can be strip-pieced and cut into squares. These are alternated between vertical and horizontal placement to create a chevron or zigzag pattern through the block. It can be a four-patch or, as here, a nine-patch, and blocks can be assembled in different colors to make a secondary pattern in a large quilt.

How to Construct a Rail Fence Block

Cutting and piecing

A | B | C

A | B | C

Cut three strips of equal width from fabrics A, B and C. Join them along their length with a 1/4 in (5 mm) seam and press the seams to the same side. Now cut across the pieced strips to create even squares.

Joining squares into strips

Stitch the pieced squares into rows, alternating the pattern vertically and horizontally. Press the seams on each row in opposite directions.

Joining rows into a block

Join the rows into a block, making sure seams match from one row to the next. Pressing the seams in opposite directions helps them to lie flat.

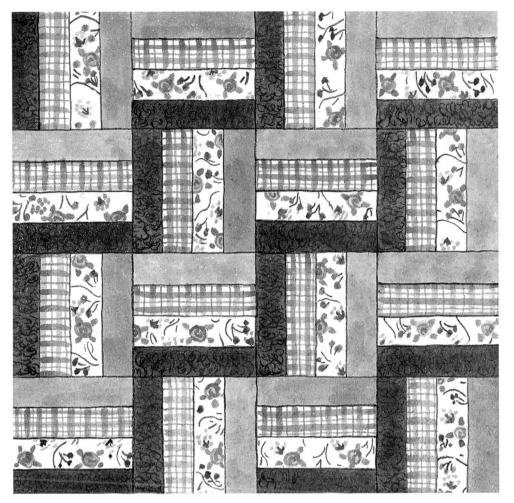

Rail Fence with Four Fabrics
Here, four different fabrics have been strip-pieced and assembled in the same way as the basic Rail Fence. The effect this creates is similarly a distinct zigzag line running diagonally through the piece, but the space between the "fences" is more varied.

Basket Weave
This block is made in a similar way to the Rail Fence block shown opposite, but uses only two fabrics. Two versions of the strips are pieced, one stitched as fabric A, then fabric B, then fabric A again, while the second is arranged BAB. Both are cut into squares as for the Rail Fence and then alternated, with the ABA squares positioned vertically and the BAB squares set horizontally. The final effect is that of a woven basket.

Log Cabin Patterns

Log Cabin

One of the favorite traditional patterns, Log Cabin is frequently used by beginners, but it is also loved by experienced quilters for its versatility and its variations. The basic block consists of a center square, traditionally made from red fabric to represent, according to legend, the hearth fire. The "logs" are strips of light and dark values which are stitched around the center square in order. The farther away from the center you go, the longer the "logs" become. This pattern is equally effective worked in silk, cotton or wool, and the strips can be cut from the same fabrics on either side or different fabrics from two color families.

_____ How to Construct a Log Cabin Block _____

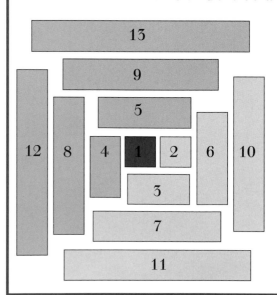

Cut strips of an equal width from your chosen fabrics, and cut the center square (1) the same width as the strips. Taking a standard $^1/4$ in (5 mm) seam allowance, join the first strip (2) and fingerpress the seam (see page 15). Add strip 3 in the same color and fingerpress again. Continue adding strips around the center, working in a clockwise direction, until the block is the desired size, fingerpressing each time so that all the seams lie in the same direction.

Chimneys and Cornerstones
This variation creates a diagonal line of squares the same size as the center squares and worked in the same color. A small square must be added to every alternate strip before it is stitched into the block.

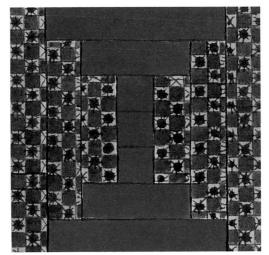

Courthouse Steps

Courthouse Steps is constructed like Log Cabin, but the lights and darks are on opposite sides of the horizontal or vertical axis. The center is composed of three identical squares sewn together and then bordered on their long sides by strips of a contrasting color.

Log Cabin Chevron

This variation is created by adding strips to the small square on two sides only. The colors are usually alternated light/dark or dark/light and added in sequence until the block reaches the desired size. Combining four blocks with the first small squares in the center creates a four-patch square made of concentric rows of strongly differentiated color. Make sure that you match the seams carefully when combining blocks.

Pineapple

This intricate-looking pattern, also called Windmill Blades, can be strip-pieced around its center block set on point, or the pieces can be cut from templates. It can be worked on a background paper or fabric pattern. Accurate cutting of the 45-degree angles is essential, but the result is often full of subsidiary patterns.

Log Cabin Diamond

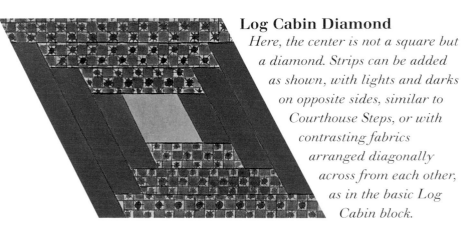

Here, the center is not a square but a diamond. Strips can be added as shown, with lights and darks on opposite sides, similar to Courthouse Steps, or with contrasting fabrics arranged diagonally across from each other, as in the basic Log Cabin block.

Off-Center Log Cabin

The beginning square here is not in the center of the block. Strips are cut both from two different colors and in two widths, narrow and wide. Assembly is the same as for the basic Log Cabin; it makes no difference to the construction whether you start with the narrow or the wide strip. Try drawing the pattern on paper beforehand if you are unsure of the finished effect. Below: When Off-Center blocks are combined, they create a very effective visual curve.

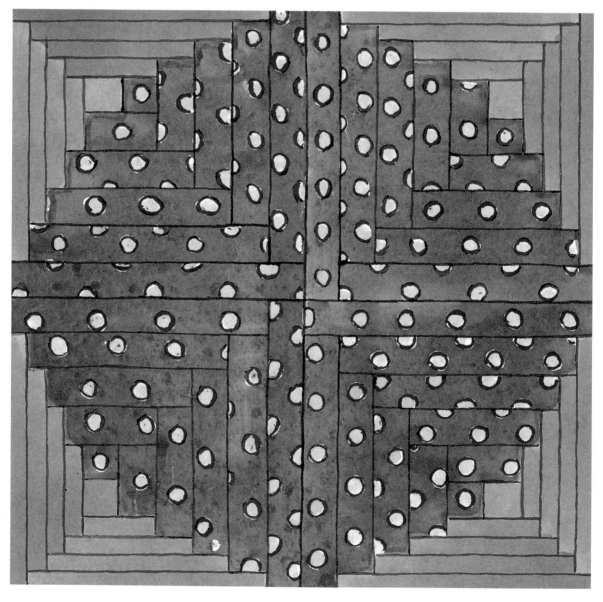

Combining Log Cabin Blocks

One of the fascinations of Log Cabin is its ability to create secondary and subsidiary patterns when it is used in combination with identical blocks. Four of the best-known are shown here, but it is worth experimenting by laying finished blocks out and moving them around until you are pleased with their arrangement. Log Cabin blocks, and most of the variations, are pieced side by side without sashing or setting blocks.

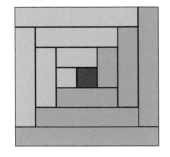

Light and Dark
Arranging blocks with four darks side by side creates this traditional setting. The secondary pattern gives square blocks of each color throughout the quilt.

Barn Raising
Here, the blocks are organized as concentric bands to make a diamond-shaped pattern. The more blocks you add, the more diamond bands you create.

Straight Furrow
With its name evoking plowed fields and country lanes, this setting creates diagonal stripes running across the quilt.

Streak of Lightning
The strong zigzag lines of this setting pattern are reminiscent of flashes of jagged lightning.

Brick & String-piecing Patterns

Brick

It is easy to see how this pattern gets its name, with the offset rectangles arranged like a brick wall. The rectangles can be cut separately and sewn into strips at random, but it is quicker to use the strip-piecing method given below. Some of the rows must be unpicked to achieve a random effect as shown, but re-sewing them in order creates the stepped pattern illustrated below right.

How to Construct a Brick Block

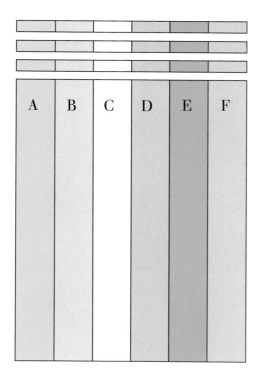

Cutting and strip-piecing

Cut strips of the desired width and stitch them together along their length, taking a $^1/4$ in (5 mm) seam allowance. Press the seams to one side, then cut across the pieced strips to make rows that are half the width of the original unsewn strips.

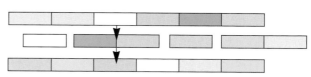

Joining rows

Arrange the cut rows in offset fashion, making sure that the short seams of each row fall in the exact center of the "bricks" in the rows above and below. To achieve a random effect, turn some rows 180 degrees, then unpick the seams at random and rearrange the pattern. Once you are happy with the overall effect, sew the unpicked seams back together again.

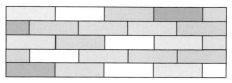

Stitching the block

Stitch the pieced rows together, aligning them carefully, and trim the edges to make a block.

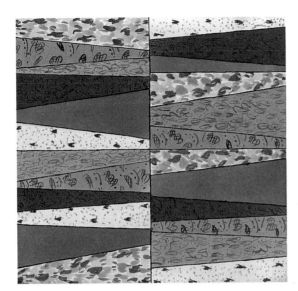

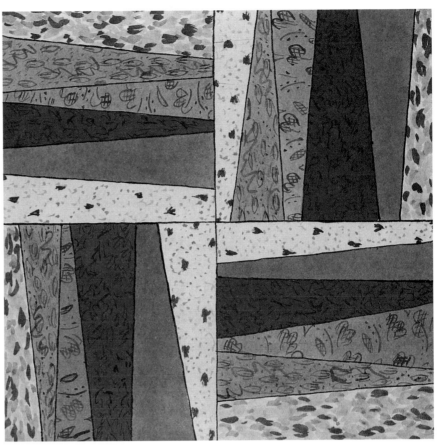

String-piecing I

String-piecing, which is not the same as strip-piecing, is perhaps the ultimate scrap-quilt technique. It is a useful way to use up the "strings" of fabric left over from rotary cutting, which are narrower at one end than at the other. The strings are sewn together along their length to make a pieced fabric in which the strips vary in width. Press the seams to one side and then cut blocks as you wish. Here, the blocks are square and have been arranged into a four-patch unit (see page 56), but more complex shapes can be used to great effect.

String-piecing II

Here, the square blocks have been arranged as a four-patch unit, but with the piecing seams at right angles to each other to make a lopsided windmill that whirls out from the center. This technique can be used very effectively in pictorial quilts, especially landscapes, but such projects need careful planning.

London Stairs

Another name for this pattern is London Steps, and step is what it does. It is made in exactly the same way as the Brick block on the left, except that the rows are placed alongside each other in the same, rather than a random, order. It also works as a scrap-quilt pattern if colors of similar values are used to make the diagonal bands of light and dark. It is essential that the short seams fall in the center of the blocks above and below.

Roman Stripe Patterns

Roman Stripe

The Roman Stripe pattern is found in Amish quilts, in which the strips are usually plain, bright colors and the triangle is black or navy blue. The blocks are joined so that the strips are always facing in the same direction, and the effect is of patterned and plain triangles facing each other. Making the strips from fabrics in shades of the same color, varying from dark to light, gives a rich, cohesive feel to a finished piece. Quilting in straight lines in the same direction as the seams of the pieced triangles keeps the simplicity of the design.

How to Construct a Roman Stripe Block

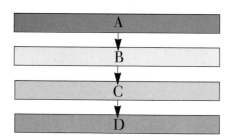

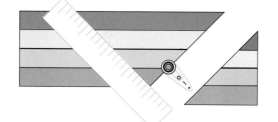

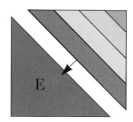

Cutting and strip-piecing

Cut a strip of each color to be used in the pieced triangle and stitch them together along the long edges, taking a standard $1/4$ in (5 mm) seam allowance. Press the seams to one side.

Cutting the triangles

Lay the pieced strips on a cutting mat and trim off one end at a 45-degree angle. Then line up the ruler to cut a right-angled triangle which has its bottom strip along the longest straight edge and the top strip in the apex. Cut a plain background triangle the same size as the pieced triangle.

Making the block

Join the pieced triangle to the background triangle by stitching along the long edges. You should be joining the straight grain of the pieced triangle to the bias edge of the plain one.

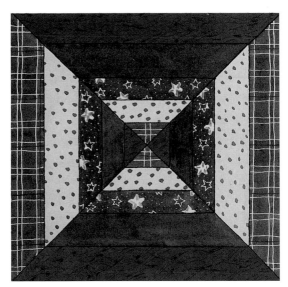

Triangle Block I

The seams of this mitered block must be matched precisely for the full effect to be seen. It requires two different pieced strips which are cut into triangles, with the narrow strips at the apex. Cut the triangles so that the longest edges are on the straight grain, but be careful when cutting and handling the bias to prevent stretching.

Triangle Block II

Here, one simple pieced strip has been cut first into two squares and then into four right-angled triangles. The right angles are placed together in the center of the block, with the same colors opposite one another, giving a lively windmill effect. In this block, the outside edges are, of necessity, cut on the bias, so handle them with great care to prevent stretching.

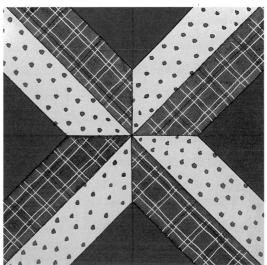

Triangle Block III

This version uses one pieced strip that is cut into right-angled triangles and combined with two triangles of plain background fabric to make the block. If this block is turned 90 degrees and repeated in an alternating sequence, an overall pattern of triangles, pieced and plain, emerges.

King's Cross

This block is made of eight pieced triangles stitched back to back and assembled like a four-patch block (see page 56). Each fabric is stitched to a strip of background fabric first, and then cut into right-angled triangles with the background fabric at the apex.

Seminole Patterns

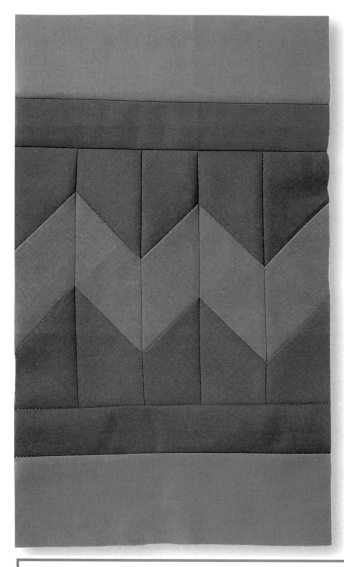

Seminole

It is easier to describe Seminole as a concept than as a pattern, because it is a stitch and cut method of constructing strips that sometimes bears little resemblance to traditional Seminole work. Originated in the early 20th century by women of the Seminole tribe of Native Americans in Florida, its jaunty geometric patterns and bright, plain colors have made it particularly popular for items such as skirts and bags. Today, tribeswomen make garments and accessories on a commercial scale. Seminole is not widely used for quilts, but the techniques can be employed for making wonderfully intricate and exotic-looking borders. The block shown here has been trimmed top and bottom, with border strips added to the chevron strip. The variations shown on these two pages are only a few of the possibilities. Try inventing your own patterns using the basic method.

How to Construct a Seminole Block

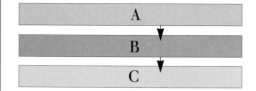

Cutting and joining strips
Cut the number of strips required and stitch together along their length, taking a $1/4$ in (5 mm) seam. Press the seams to one side. Repeat to make another identical pieced strip.

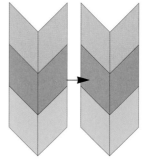

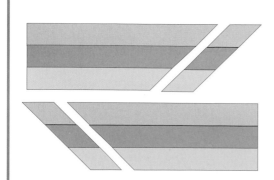

Cutting strips
Cut the first pieced strip across the diagonal at a 45-degree angle into short equal lengths. Repeat the process with the second pieced strip, this time cutting in the opposite direction to the first.

Making the Seminole pattern
Stitch the short lengths together in pairs along their longest edges, matching seams as you work, to create a chevron pattern. Stitch the pairs together into rows, trimming top and bottom points if desired.

Single Chevron

The technique for this block is the same as for the block opposite, but the top and bottom strips have been alternated, which has the effect of visually reinforcing the zigzag stripe. The borders at the top and bottom of the block are added after the chevron strip is stitched and trimmed.

Diamonds

This block is most easily made by strip-piecing five strips. The two plain outer strips are four to five times as wide as the three inner ones, which are all the same width. The pieced strip is cut into rows the same width as the original inner strips and then stitched together by staggering the center squares to create a diagonal strip. The block is squared off on all four sides.

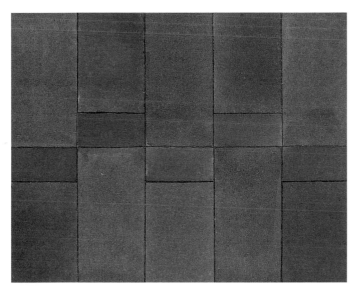

Steps

This simple Seminole pattern is made from three strips of different widths that are sewn together along their length and then cut into even rows in the usual way. By turning alternate strips 180 degrees, the stepped pattern in the middle is created when the strips are stitched together again.

Double Chevron

Here, four strips of equal width are joined and then cut apart on an angle (this is 45 degrees). If the strip is folded in half with right sides together along the short edge, the cut strips automatically become mirror images that can be alternated and stitched back together.

Irish Chain Patterns

Irish Chain

Double Irish Chain, the version shown here, is probably the best-known of this family, in which a pieced block alternates with a plain one to create a diagonal pattern that runs throughout the quilt. While no evidence has been found to show that the pattern originated in Ireland, it has been widely used in Britain and America since the 18th century. All the variations are constructed from two different blocks, one intricately pieced from small squares and the other either a plain square or a very simple pieced block. The blank areas created by the plain squares provide scope for quilting or appliqué.

How to Construct Irish Chain Blocks

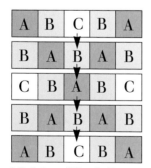

Making Block I

Cut strips and join into three arrangements: ABCBA, BABAB and CBABC (see page 34). Cut across the pieced strips in rows and stitch together as shown.

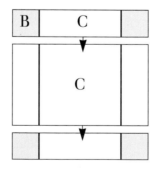

Making Block II

Cut a center square from C, four corner squares from B and four strips the same width as the corners from C. Join into three rows, then join the rows into a block.

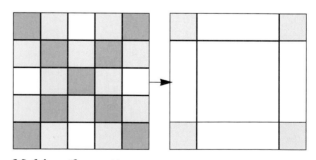

Making the pattern

Taking a standard $1/4$ in (5 mm) seam allowance, join the two pieced blocks along one edge, matching seams carefully as you work.

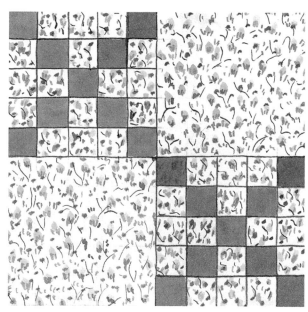

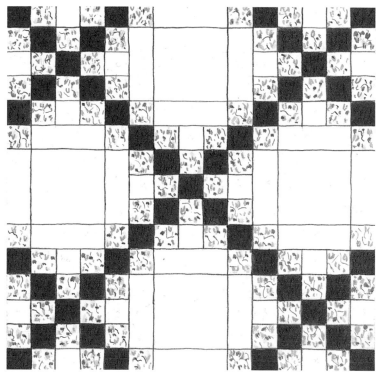

Double Irish Chain

This block shows the effect of combining several of the blocks shown on the opposite page into a traditional Double Irish Chain pattern. Each additional set of blocks creates a longer chain from the center and more chains developing in opposite corners.

Single Irish Chain

This version of Irish Chain is made up of five-by-five square blocks in two colors combined with plain unpieced blocks. This gives a more intricate chain effect than the double nine-patch shown on page 35, but still provides a smooth unpieced surface for quilting.

Triple Irish Chain

This highly traditional version is even more intricate. The two blocks are both pieced five-by-five blocks: one is pieced in the same sequence as Block I opposite, while the other is strip-pieced in the same way but in a different order – BCACB, CAAAC and AAAAA. The third, or triple, chain is interrupted occasionally by the central chain arriving from the opposite diagonal, but the overall effect is still of a third chain outside of the double one. This pattern is more difficult to quilt in the background block because of the pieced seams, but even so, simple motifs can be used to great effect.

Squares & Triangles

Squares are one of the easiest shapes to piece, and right-angled triangles can be cut simply and accurately from squares. Using a rotary cutter, you can cut strips that can be subdivided into squares and then into right-angled triangles, known as triangle patches.

Many of the designs based on these shapes are traditional American or British patterns, with wonderfully evocative names that conjure up the harsh rural lives of the women who first made them: Bear's Paw, Wild Goose Chase and Sawtooth are a few well-known ones.

Trip Around the World is a pattern based entirely on squares. The cotton fabrics overprinted with gold used in this version (1995) give the quilt a warm, rich quality.

Quilt Gallery

SQUARES ARE thought by many to have been the basis for the oldest patchwork patterns. Certainly squares, rectangles and strips of cloth are the easiest shapes to join together, since they are all stitched using only straight seams.

The simplest square pattern is probably the one-patch design, made traditionally of randomly placed squares. In a version known as Charm Quilt, all the patches (usually, but not necessarily, squares) are the same size, but each is made from a different fabric. Square patches are sewn together into strips, which are then joined in rows to make a quilt, but diamonds and triangles can be

used. In the popular Postage Stamp pattern, each square – as befits its name – is tiny. Historical examples usually show the use of many different scraps of fabric. Some are arranged randomly, as though the pieces were added on as they became available, while others – often consisting of hundreds or even thousands of individual minute squares – are carefully planned to create amazingly intricate designs.

Other patterns based entirely on strategically positioned squares include Trip Around the World, in which diagonal rows of color encircle the middle square, and Sunshine and Shadow, a favorite Amish design, in which the shading of the fabrics from row to row moves from dark to light. Both of these patterns can be pieced more quickly – and more accurately – than in the past by rotary-cutting strips and joining them in a particular order, then slicing across the seams and re-joining them in off-set rows. The same method can be used to create patterns similar to Bargello or Florentine embroidery, and to make waves of color arranged across the quilt.

In four-patch designs, four squares of the same size are joined into a repeating pattern to make a larger piece. A large number of more intricate patterns, in which each square is made up of various

Pinwheel

This Ohio Amish crib quilt (c.1925–35) has been worked in typical plain colors to make random pinwheel blocks. The arrangement of the colors has created a secondary pattern of squares on point within the quilt . Each triangle is outline quilted, while the wide blue outer border is quilted in simple parallel lines. The red binding matches the inner border.

combinations of other shapes – from triangles to curves – are assembled on the simple four-patch principle. Double Four-patch patterns abound, usually made with a small four-patch placed in two opposite corners of a larger four-patch block. Nine-patch patterns are also based on squares, but because they are put together using the strip-piecing method, most of them have been covered in the previous chapter. However, several of the patterns – included in this chapter because they are made entirely of squares and triangles – involve nine-patch piecing.

Squares can also be used to create octagonal shapes for the pattern known as Snowball. The piecing is done by placing a small square in each corner of a larger one and stitching across the diagonal of the small square. The excess triangle is then cut away. The same method can be applied to Bow Tie, in which four small squares meet in the center of a four-patch block.

UNIFORM QUILTS

Although traditionally quilts made from squares appear to have been less popular in Britain and Europe than they were in North America, one group of magnificent examples from the late 19th century survives today. Known as Uniform Quilts,

Sawtooth

This 19th-century quilt from York County, Pennsylvania, with its intricate sawtooth-edged pattern was never used – perhaps it was part of a hope chest. Somewhat unusually for the time, it is signed on the back "I.R. Sterret No. 8". The cotton batting still contained seeds when it was acquired by the American Museum in Britain. The floral, feather and leaf quilting is very neatly stitched.

they were assembled mainly by British soldiers and sailors. They were made from the heavy but colorful woollen fabrics used to make the military uniforms of the day. Most of these patterns are highly geometric, and while they were too heavy and inflexible to quilt, they would have

English Medallion Quilt
This beautiful British quilt from the 1880s uses squares in almost all of its complex elements. The central square medallion is made from 25 pieced Ohio Stars, and each of the four inner borders contains a corner square. Made in cotton, the quilt incorporates several different patterned fabrics and is finished with a wide greenish-gold outer border. It is quilted all over with the traditional wineglass pattern that occurs on many quilts from the North-east of England.

provided the maker with a warm cover, as well as hours of enjoyable work.

TRIANGLES

Cutting squares from corner to corner gives right-angled triangles, known as triangle patches. Although these are trickier to work, since one seam must be stitched along the bias, they broaden the scope for creating interesting patterns within the format of the block. Combining right-angled triangles with squares and strips to make patches for four-patch and nine-patch

blocks has provided quilt makers with ideas for patchwork patterns for centuries.

Many well-known and very effective four-patch patterns, such as Pinwheel and its cousin Windmill, Broken Dishes, Cotton Reel and Streak of Lightning, use patches consisting of two contrasting triangles stitched together along the long side and combined into blocks. Simple nine-patch blocks offer even more variety, from Friendship Star, Shoofly and Ohio Star to Maple Leaf and Bear's Paw. The sawtooth pattern that is used to great effect on borders and in sashing is made of alternating light and dark right-angled triangles, fashioned in a similar way to the block known as Sawtooth. Don't forget that triangles can be turned on point, as in Flying Geese, which can be used for borders or made into strips that can be assembled into "strippy" quilts. Amish Bars quilts often have alternating bars made using the Flying Geese pattern. Equilateral (60-degree) and isosceles triangles are also used, especially in the Thousand Pyramids design. Rows of triangle shapes are joined with the points and bases alternating, and the resulting strips are sewn together to make the quilt. Light and dark colors can be organized to make fascinating and intricate patterns within the piece.

Triangles are used to make many of the familiar star patterns, and form the basis of many of the Tree of Life and Pine Tree designs that were popular with American quilters in the latter part of the 19th century. Indeed, many of the tree variations that make naturalistic flower forms are also based on triangles, as are a number of Basket patterns in which the handle is constructed from small triangles while the basket itself is formed from larger ones.

A trip to a museum with a collection of quilts, or a look in any book about antique quilts, will reveal squares and triangles used in myriad fascinating ways, and studying them will repay dividends.

Maple Leaf

In this patriotic version of the popular Maple Leaf pattern, bought new by the author at an auction in Lancaster County, Pennsylvania, in 1994, the nine-patch blocks are turned on point, separated by plain white squares and edged with white triangles. Narrow parallel lines of quilting delineate the leaf blocks, while the white spaces are filled with finely quilted roses. The border is decorated with interlocking hearts.

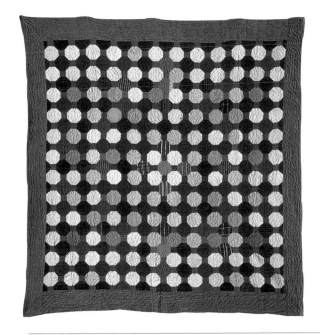

Snowball

Known as the Ovington quilt, this version of the Snowball pattern was made (c.1900) by Mrs Sybil Heslop from Ovington, Northumberland. She was well-known in the Scottish Borders country north of her home, where she often visited the local woollen mills collecting "fents", or samples, of the flannels and suitings from which this quilt is made. The reverse side is also pieced – this time from squares – and the entire reversible quilt, including the bottle-green border, has been quilted in the wineglass pattern.

Four-patch Patterns

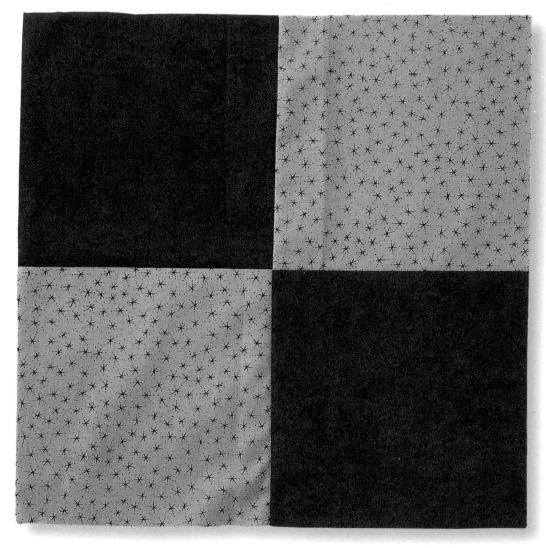

Four-patch

This block, made of four basic squares, is probably the simplest of all pieced patchwork shapes. It is straightforward to make, but it also provides the basis for a myriad of blocks. The basic pattern relies for its effectiveness on a strong contrast between light and dark color values. Different shades of a single color, or two solid-colored or two coordinated prints, can be striking, although the use of one plain and one patterned fabric is more usual. The basic method for combining the blocks is given below, but a quicker version involving strip-piecing is explained on page 34.

How to Construct a Four-patch Block

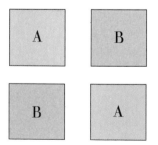

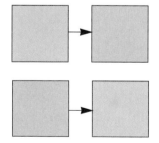

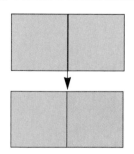

Cutting
Cut four squares, two from fabric A and two from fabric B.

Joining pairs
Taking a standard $1/4$ in (5 mm) seam, stitch each A square to its corresponding B square.

Joining rows of pairs
Match the seams of the pairs and stitch them with fabric A opposite fabric B.

Rainbow Flower

Four different fabrics are used in this double four-patch block. The top right and bottom left four-patch units are identical, while the other two are both different, but are each constructed using three squares of one fabric plus one square of another. If you turn the block on its point, it becomes an abstract tulip which can be combined with setting triangles and/or sashing to make an effective simple quilt.

Four-patch plus Squares

Here, the pieced blocks are simple four-patch units that have been combined with plain squares, creating a diagonal chain within the block and providing scope for quilting in the plain squares. The pieced units can be chain-pieced (see page 17) and then combined to make larger blocks, or they can be strip-pieced (see page 34) to make small four-patches.

Sixteen-patch

This block is also known as double four-patch and, as shown, is the result of combining four of the basic four-patch blocks opposite. It creates a checkerboard effect that can, of course, be emphasized by the use of very dark and very light colors. It can be alternated with plain blocks of the same size or offset by turning the block on point to create right-angled diamonds.

Postage Stamp Patterns

Postage Stamp

The tiny squares that make up this pattern are postage-stamp size, hence its name. Traditionally, Postage Stamp squares are placed at random and cut from large numbers of fabrics, making this technique ideal for scrap quilts. This version, however, is strip-pieced from nine different fabrics, with a few extra squares thrown in to create a random effect. The technique was widely used by quiltmakers in the United States during the 1930s, when the Great Depression made frugality both a virtue and a necessity.

The instructions below have been devised as a time-saving strip-piecing method, but it is possible to make a Postage Stamp quilt by cutting individual squares, stitching them into rows and then stitching the rows together as strips.

How to Construct a Postage Stamp Block

Cutting and strip-piecing

Cut narrow strips of each fabric and stitch together along their length, taking a $^1/4$ in (5 mm) seam allowance. Press the seams to one side. Cut the pieced strips into even rows the same width and turn some of them 180 degrees to achieve a random effect.

Joining rows

Unpick squares in some rows and move the pieces around until you create a pattern that pleases you, then stitch the unpicked rows back together again. To create a block, stitch the pieced rows together, matching the short seams carefully on all rows.

Trip Around the World

This popular pattern can be made from just a few fabrics that echo each other as they radiate out from the center, or a dozen or more different colors, including shades of the same color. Another version of this design, Sunshine and Shadow, in which the bands of color vary from light to dark and back again, is a favorite pattern of Amish quiltmakers, who use traditional plain colors. Squares of 4–5 in (10–12.5 cm) can be stitched to create a quick quilt, but smaller ones – 2–2 ¹/₂ in (5–6.5 cm) – make an altogether richer-looking piece.

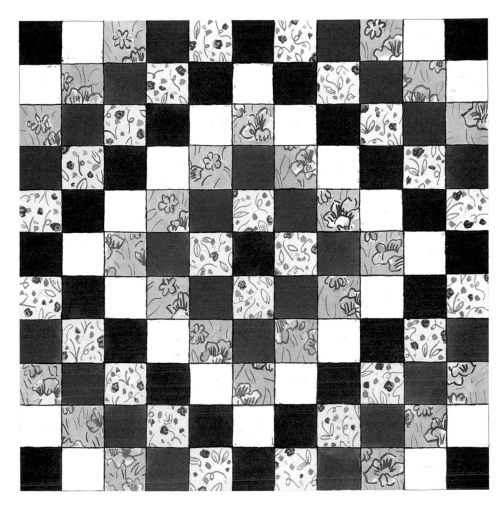

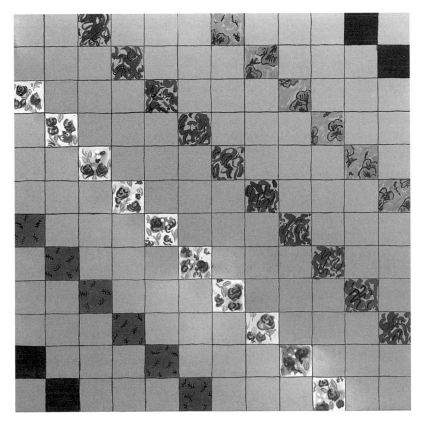

Kite Tails

If you imagine these diagonal rows of color running through a sky-blue background, you can see how this pattern got its name. The color blocks can, of course, be turned to run across the opposite diagonal. Both Kite Tails and Trip Around the World (above) can be assembled using quick strip-piecing methods that involve unpicking seams and re-stitching in the correct order (see opposite), or the squares can be joined in rows that are then sewn together. Whichever method is used, it is important that each seam is matched precisely.

Friendship Star Patterns

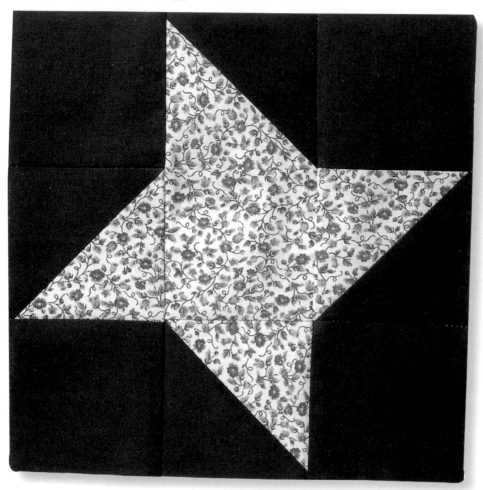

Friendship Star

This simple nine-patch block forms the basis of a number of interesting patterns. The triangle patches are arranged into a four-pointed star which gives the block the appearance of tumbling or whirling through the air. It can be combined with plain squares of the same size to create a very simple but vibrant quilt — a dark blue background, combined with a light fabric overprinted with gold or silver, gives the look of a clear night sky very effectively.

How to Construct a Friendship Star Block

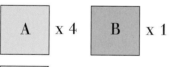

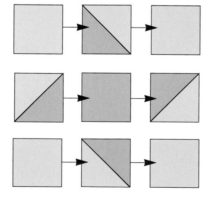

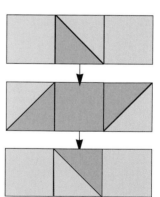

Cutting and making squares

To make the triangle patches, cut two squares each from fabric A and B. Cut them along one diagonal to make eight triangles. Taking a ¹/4 in (5 mm) seam, stitch together to make four matching squares. Then cut one square the same size from fabric A and four squares from fabric B.

Joining squares

Arrange the nine squares as shown and stitch together in rows. Press the seams to one side.

Joining rows

Stitch the three rows together to form a block, matching seams carefully as you work.

Milky Way

The Milky Way pattern is a well-named galaxy of Friendship Stars made more complex by the four-patch squares in the corners between the points. The block is more complicated than it first looks. It is not just a simple arrangement of Friendship Star blocks, but a series of contrasting Friendship Stars that lie next to each other in rows. The four-patch squares that fill the spaces between the points emphasize the adjoining stars and are alternated in two directions, giving even more vitality to the design. It is probably easiest to begin by making the four-patch squares (see page 56) and triangle patches (see opposite). You can then assemble them into rows and include the plain, unpieced squares that form the center of the stars.

Nine-patch Star

This simple Friendship Star is enlivened by the use of triangle patches in the corners, with the diagonal seams radiating out from the center.

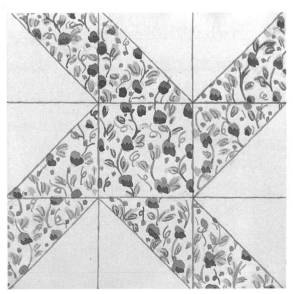

Formal Garden

This block is also called Box, perhaps because it is reminiscent of the box hedges found in formal gardens. It is another simple Friendship Star, made from the same elements as the Nine-patch Star (left), but using only two colors.

Broken Dishes Patterns

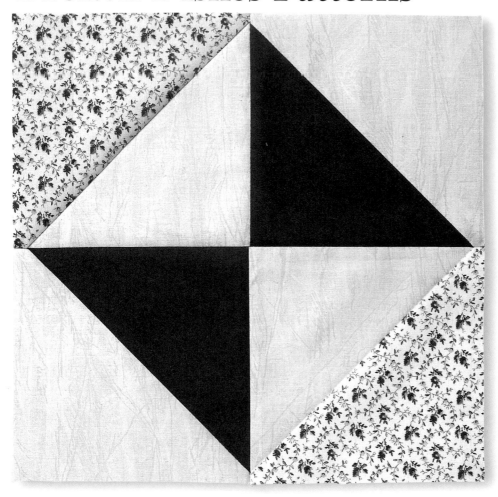

Broken Dishes

This simple four-patch pattern is derived solely from right-angled triangles and uses three fabrics. When blocks are combined, the effect − or so the legend goes − is of a pile of broken dishes on the floor. It is certainly fragmented, but the pattern is much more attractive than the image conjured up by that description. It is traditionally made into units of four blocks and alternated with plain background blocks. If each unit is turned a different way, the broken dishes look is enhanced even further.

How to Construct a Broken Dishes Block

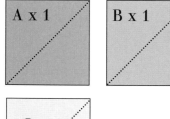

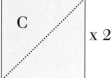

Cutting

Cut four squares for each block: one each of fabrics A and B and two of fabric C. On the wrong side of each square, draw a diagonal line from corner to corner in one direction only.

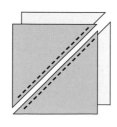

Making triangle patches (quick method)

Placing right sides together, arrange the squares in pairs − A with C, and B with C − matching diagonal lines. Align the presser foot along the diagonal line and stitch a $^1/4$ in (5 mm) seam first on the left-hand side of the line and then on the right-hand side. Cut along the marked line very carefully ,then press the squares open.

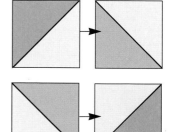

Joining squares into a block

Arrange the four pieced squares as shown and stitch together in pairs, taking a $^1/4$ in (5 mm) seam allowance. Matching the seams in the center carefully, stitch the pairs into a block.

Peace and Plenty

This double four-patch is composed entirely of right-angled triangles. The center is a basic Pinwheel (see page 66), which is surrounded by units in which colors are alternated in an unusual way.

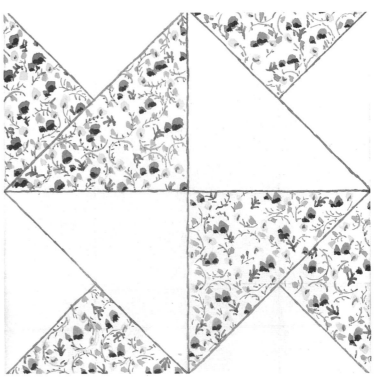

Southern Belle

This simple four-patch has a center identical to that of Broken Dishes, but the outside triangles of each patch are made of right-angled triangles. Its slanted lines give the block a whirligig look.

Fancy Stripe

Another double four-patch, Fancy Stripe is made of 16 identical triangle patches arranged to make a striped block of color in the center. It can be turned on point, as here, and squared up with setting triangles, or set as a square, creating small squares of color where the corners meet.

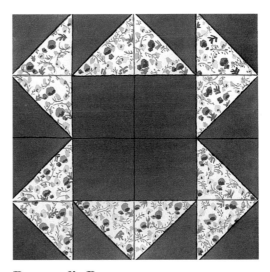

Buzzard's Roost

This double four-patch, with its fanciful name, has four plain squares in the middle bordered by triangle patches on all sides. These are arranged back to back to create larger triangles of color that point in all four directions.

Ohio Star Patterns

Ohio Star

Ohio Star is a popular nine-patch block with countless variations. In its simplest form, it consists of five plain and four pieced squares of the same size. The example shown here is made up of eight patterned triangles that match the center patch, and eight plain triangles made from the same fabric as the four corner patches. These pieced blocks are usually alternated with plain ones, although some quilts use simple sashing (see page 18) to separate the blocks.

How to Construct an Ohio Star Block

Cutting and making squares

For the triangle patches, cut two squares from each fabric and cut them twice along the diagonal. Each pieced square consists of two triangles of each fabric that face each other at the apex. Stitch the triangle patches (see page 15) and press the seams. Cut four corner squares from A and one center square from B the same size as the pieced squares.

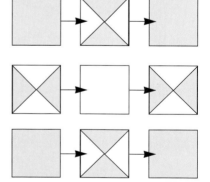

Joining squares

Arrange the pieced and plain squares as shown and stitch together in rows, taking a $^1/4$ in (5 mm) seam. Press the seams to one side.

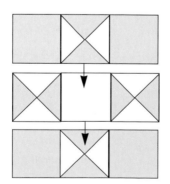

Joining rows

Join the three rows together to form a block, matching corner seams carefully. Press the long seams to one side.

Country Farm

This variation is created using four fabrics. The center square is a basic four-patch made from two squares each of light and dark fabric placed opposite one another. The inner points of the triangle patches are made from one triangle of each of the same two fabrics. The outer points of the triangle patches match the fabric used for the corner squares, while the star points are made from a fourth fabric. The block is made by first stitching the five pieced patches and then combining them with the four plain corner patches, as for Ohio Star.

Variable Star

This variation uses three contrasting fabrics. The central square is made from the same fabric as the inner points of the triangle patches to give the appearance of a square turned on point. The construction is the same as Ohio Star.

Card Basket

Four fabrics are used here to create a star shape with a double diamond in the middle. The center square consists of a square on point, with the corners added in a contrasting fabric that matches the inner points of the surrounding triangle patches. The center square is made from the same fabric as the double star points of the triangle patches. Each corner square is made of two right-angled triangles in coordinating fabrics; the inner fabric of each matches the fabric used in the outer points of the triangle patches.

Pinwheel Patterns

Pinwheel

This popular pattern, also called Windmill, has an even more descriptive, and probably older, name of Flutter Blades. It is one of the simplest four-patch blocks to construct and, like so many simple shapes, has endless variations. Blocks can be set side by side with colors alternating to create a mass of turning triangles, or they can be combined with plain blocks or emphasized with sashing. Made from random scraps, the pattern takes on an entirely different feel, but it is almost invariably full of vitality.

How to Construct a Pinwheel Block

Making triangle patches

Cut two squares from each fabric and cut them once along the diagonal. Taking a ¹/4 in (5 mm) seam allowance, join one fabric A triangle to a fabric B triangle along the diagonal to make a square. Repeat with the other triangles and press the seams to one side. The bias seam stretches easily, so handle it carefully when stitching and pressing.

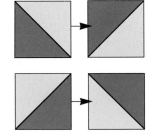 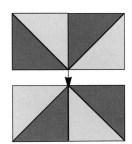

Joining squares into a block

Arrange the triangle patches in the order shown and stitch into rows. Then join the rows together, matching seams carefully at the center. This is easier to do if you pin the points together precisely and stitch carefully over the pin.

Double Pinwheel

Here, one set of blades is pieced from two right-angled triangles. The smaller blades begin at the center of each side, while the larger ones start from the corners. A different choice of colors would make the larger blades more prominent, whereas here the smaller blades dominate the block. A variation of this variation, called Turnstile, uses the same color for the larger blades and the background triangles, but is otherwise identical.

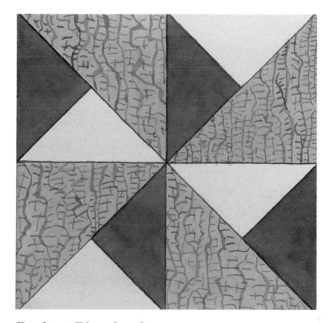

Broken Pinwheel

The construction of this block is the same as Double Pinwheel (above), but the colors of the smaller blades are alternated. The pieced triangles can be made from two pieced squares that are cut across the seam to give two sets of mirror images.

Trailing Star

This variation of Pinwheel is a double four-patch (see page 57), in which all the units are constructed as triangle patches and then stitched in the order shown. The additional layer of diagonal color adds to the feeling of movement.

Shoofly Patterns

Shoofly

Shoofly — or Shoo-fly or Shoo Fly — is a simple but effective nine-patch block. It remains a popular design and can be found in everything from sampler quilts and cushions to miniature and crib quilts. The four corner patches are triangle patches made in contrasting fabrics, with the center square matching the inner triangles, and the surrounding four squares matching the outer triangles. The novelty striped fabric used for this block gives a vertical feel — if the stripes were alternated or set on the diagonal, the block would look very different.

_____ How to Construct a Shoofly Block _____

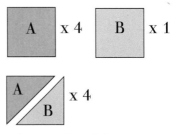

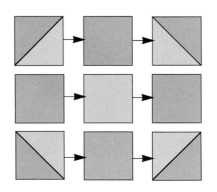

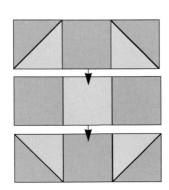

Cutting and making squares

Cut two squares from each fabric and cut them once along the diagonal to make eight triangles. Take a triangle of each fabric and stitch to a triangle of contrasting fabric to make four squares. Cut four squares from A and one from B the same size as the pieced squares.

Joining squares

Arrange the nine patches as shown and stitch together in rows (see page 34 for How to Construct a Nine-patch Block).

Joining rows

Stitch the three rows together to form a block, matching seams carefully so that the points of the inner triangles don't get caught in the seam allowance.

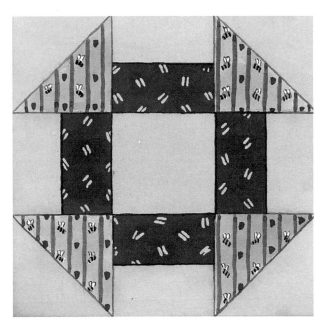

Churn Dash

Churn Dash is one of the patterns that looks recognizably like its namesake. It is constructed like Shoofly except that the four corner units are triangle patches, while the squares in between are pieced from two strips of the same width. It is an effective pattern to use for making a scrap quilt.

Calico Puzzle

This simple variation is identical in its construction to Shoofly, but the corner patches are made from the main fabric plus a second contrasting one, and the diagonal seams point into the center square. This pattern would be suitable for a scrap quilt, provided that the second contrasting fabric remains the same throughout, with the main fabric and the contrasting fabric used for the plain squares.

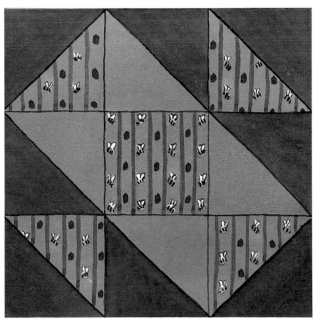

Box Kite

In this simple nine-patch block, all the outer squares are triangle patches — the corner patches are made from a triangle of main fabric and a triangle of background, while the squares in between are made from a triangle of background fabric and a triangle of contrasting fabric.

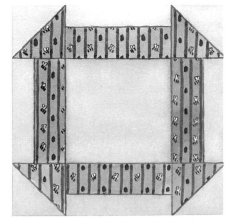

Hole in the Barn Door

This block is a variation of Churn Dash (above), in which the center square is twice the width of the corner squares and the strip-pieced outer units are twice as long as they are wide. This pattern is found in plain colors in traditional Amish quilts, perhaps because the size of the center block gives scope for intricate quilting – a typical feature of Amish work.

Maple Leaf Patterns

Maple Leaf

This simple nine-patch block, of which there are many versions, looks like its namesake. The stem patch can be pieced, or the stem can be applied as a separate piece by hand or machine. Blocks are usually sashed or alternated with plain blocks to emphasize the leaf shape. There are quilts made with leaves of every conceivable color; the most beautiful one I have ever seen was in earthy greens, yellows and browns, all overprinted with gold. The pattern works whether the fabric is printed or plain. Setting the blocks in different directions creates the impression of falling leaves.

How to Construct a Maple Leaf Block

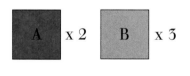

Cutting and making squares

Cut and stitch four triangle patches using fabrics A and B (see page 60 and page 62). Cut two plain A and three plain B squares the same size as the finished pieced squares.

Making the stem

Cut a strip of contrasting fabric for the stem and topstitch it to one A square across the diagonal.

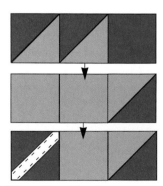

Making the block

Arrange the patches as shown. Stitch the squares together in three rows, then join the rows into a block (see How to Construct a Nine-patch Block, page 34).

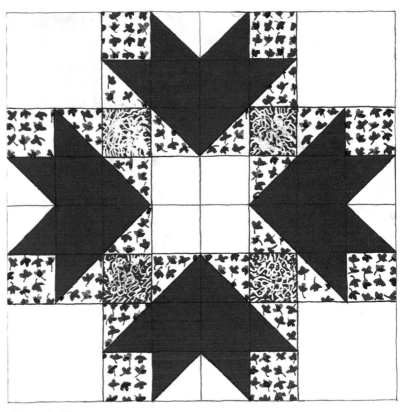

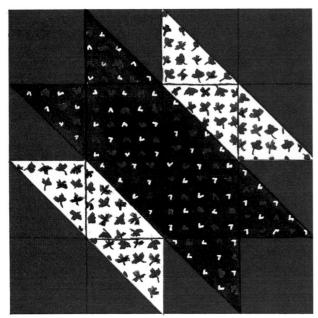

Anvil

Shaped like an anvil, this block is probably easier to construct than Maple Leaf. It is a double four-patch (see page 57) which is basically a mirror image of the "leaf" half of the basic block. The four corners and two of the middle units are unpieced squares; the remaining units are triangle patches. The block can be assembled as four four-patch units which are then joined, or in four rows each containing four squares.

Crow's Foot

Based on the same shapes as Maple Leaf, this is a more complex block. It is most easily approached as a double-double four-patch, with the corner units either unpieced squares, as shown, or assembled as separate four-patch units. All the elements are either simple squares or triangle patches.

Lilies

This attractive flower block is straightforward to make and the lilies themselves are basically the same shape as Maple Leaf, but the construction is different. The center is a basic nine-patch (see page 34) turned on point, with the large corner triangles added all around. The spiky "petals" of the flowers, formed from plain unpieced squares and triangle patches, can be constructed in rows and added to the edges like a pieced border (see page 19).

Snail's Trail Patterns

Snail's Trail

The twists and turns of Snail's Trail make it clear how it got its name. It is an interesting block to construct, with its layers of triangles sewn on in such a way that they form visual not actual curves, but its real intrigue lies in its pattern when blocks are combined. It can be joined in several ways, with each new block enlarging the "trail" of color that winds through the piece. It is highly effective in just two colors, but the contrast between light and dark must be very strong.

How to Construct a Snail's Trail Block

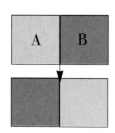

Center squares

Cut four small squares, two from fabric A and two from B, and stitch them together alternating colors, or strip-piece the unit (see page 56). Cut templates for the triangles. The block above uses four different sizes.

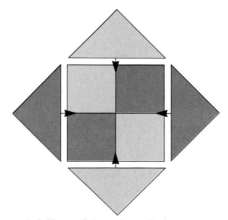

Adding side triangles

Add the first layer of triangles, stitching the dark and then the light fabrics on opposite sides of the center square.

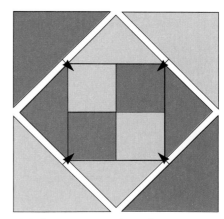

Adding more triangles

Continue adding layers of triangles as before, increasing the size and working around the block with opposite darks, then opposite lights.

Monkey Wrench

This pattern is constructed in exactly the same way as Snail's Trail. Here, it is shown made in four different fabrics, which emphasize the shape of its curve and make it look like the head of the tool that gives it its name. Using more than two fabrics creates even more possibilities for making unusual patterns when blocks are combined to make a large piece.

Rough Sea

With its storm-tossed look, Rough Sea is constructed on the same principle as Snail's Trail, but the center square of each block is made of four right-angled triangles instead of four small squares. The second layer uses triangles of the same size. The outside shapes are parallelograms and squares.

Wheel of Fortunc

This traditional wheel pattern is related to Snail's Trail, not in its construction but in its use of triangles and straight-sided shapes to create a visual curve. Despite its complex looks, it is a straightforward four-patch block involving only four shapes.

Jacob's Ladder Patterns

Jacob's Ladder

A number of traditional patterns, either devised or used by colonists in North America, were given biblical names that reflected the religious nature of their daily lives. The pieces needed to make a Jacob's Ladder block are quite small, so this pattern has the advantage of allowing the maker to be frugal with fabric and still create an intricate and appealing design. The block is a nine-patch in which alternate blocks in each row are four-patch squares, using two of the three fabrics. The remaining four patches are triangle patches made from one of the four-patch fabrics and a third, contrasting, one.

How to Construct a Jacob's Ladder Block

Cutting

Cut even strips of fabrics A and B and join together along their length, then cut across the pieced strips to make short two-patch lengths. Cut two squares each of fabrics B and C for making the triangle patches.

Making the squares

Alternating the fabrics as shown, make five four-patch units by stitching two two-patch lengths together. Use fabrics B and C to make four triangle patches, either using the method of cutting, then stitching right-angled triangles (see page 60) or the quick method on page 62.

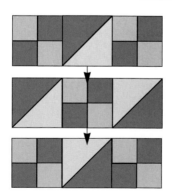

Assembling the block

Arrange the pieced squares as shown and stitch together in rows. Sew the three rows together, matching seams carefully.

Crosses and Losses

Could the fanciful name of this variation also be based on the biblical tradition? It is a double four-patch (see page 57), based entirely on squares and triangle patches, assembled to make two small and one large cross.

Railroad

This more complicated-looking block is simply a double nine-patch (see page 35), with the look of a train track running diagonally across it. It is made, like Jacob's Ladder, almost entirely of unpieced squares — only the eight units that form the strong diagonal line of the "track" are pieced triangle patches.

Double Cross

This double four-patch is similar to the one above, but the two smaller cross shapes are turned in the same direction as the larger one, and the two opposite corner units are also made from triangle patches. In another, very similar variation, the corner units are all unpieced squares.

Hovering Hawks

This is another double four-patch with a definite diagonal emphasis. It was named, no doubt, by a quilter given to flights of fancy, hawks being hard to see in the block's configuration. It is, like all the other blocks on this page, made from unpieced

squares and triangle patches, and demonstrates once again the amazing versatility of these shapes.

Pine Tree Patterns

Pine Tree

Tree motifs, almost infinite in their variety, have always been a part of design. Most of the pieced blocks depicting trees are formed from squares and triangles, and some are very complex. The relatively simple example shown here is a five-by-five patch block in which most of the squares are made from right-angled triangles. Stems can be applied or embroidered, as for Maple Leaf (page 70), or pieced as here. To make a veritable forest from Pine Tree blocks, the squares look best turned on point so that they stand upright, but effective patterns can be created from blocks set square as well.

How to Construct a Pine Tree Block

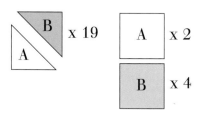

Cutting and making squares

Make 19 triangle patches (see page 60 and page 62) using fabrics A and B. Cut two squares from fabric A and four from fabric B, all the same size as the finished pieced squares.

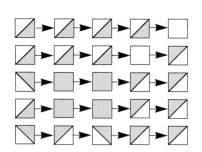

Making rows

Arrange the 25 squares as shown and join them into five rows, each containing five squares.

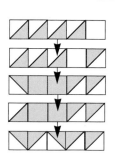

Joining rows

Matching seams and points carefully, stitch the rows together to form a block.

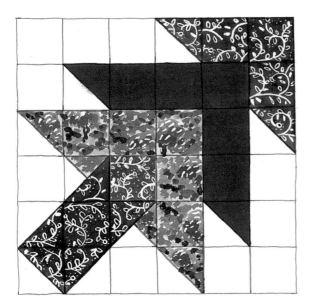

Tall Pine Tree

Most patchwork patterns depicting plant forms finish up on the diagonal, and this one is no exception. Made from squares and triangle patches, it works well whether it is set square, as here, or turned on point. Each "branch" can be made from a different fabric, as shown, or they can all be the same.

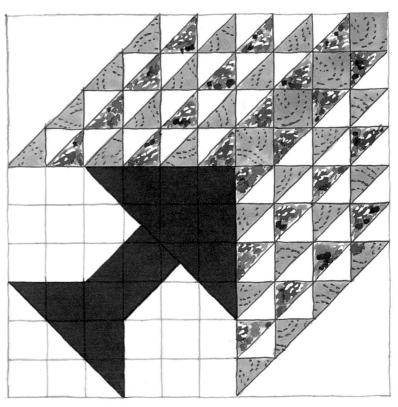

Tree of Paradise

This motif, complex though it looks, is still based entirely on small squares and triangle patches. It is best to make the triangle patches first and then piece each row separately. The block can be very effective as the medallion in the center of a simple quilt.

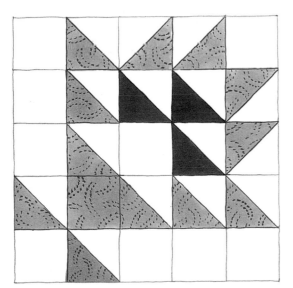

Fruit Basket

A number of the myriad basket patterns work on the same principle as the tree motifs. This five-by-five patch block is based on the familiar square and triangle patches, and should be assembled in rows after the required number of triangle patches have been made.

Evergreen

This variation is different because it is made from pieced strips stitched in rows and trimmed to make a square. Unlike the other variations shown here, it does not work well if it is set square, but it can, of course, be made into a square by adding setting triangles on all four sides.

Bow Tie Patterns

Bow Tie

The Bow Tie pattern, looking very much like its name, is a straightforward four-patch block based on large squares, with corner triangles that meet in the center to form the "knot". Made in two colors, or shades of the same two colors, it creates a very dramatic abstract design. It works equally well as a scrap quilt in which each bow is made from a different fabric, while the background remains the same throughout. The cut-off triangles may seem wasteful of fabric – put them in a box to use in a miniature quilt.

How to Construct a Bow Tie Block

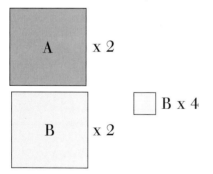

Cutting

Cut two squares from fabric A and two from fabric B. Cut four small squares for the center from fabric B and draw a diagonal line on the wrong side of each one.

Adding the corners

Place a small square in one corner of each large square, with right sides together, and stitch along the marked diagonal line. Cut away the excess triangles, leaving a 1/4 in (5 mm) seam allowance, and press the seams toward the middle.

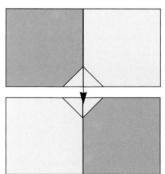

Making the block

Join the squares to make a four-patch block (see page 56). The pieced corners must point into the center, and the seams must be matched carefully.

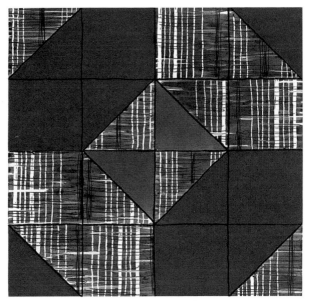

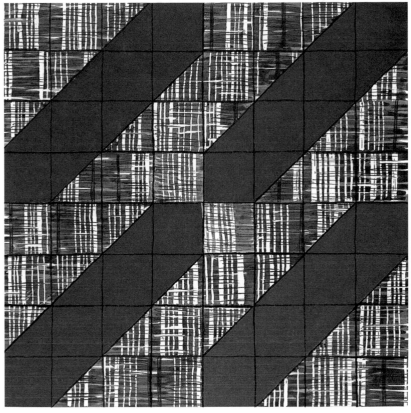

Robbing Peter to Pay Paul

This is one of several patterns bearing this name, some of which use curved instead of straight shapes (see Curve Patterns, page 104). All depend on light and dark color combinations for the positive/negative effect. Viewing this block along either diagonal gives a mirror image, which is unusual since most blocks mirror each other along one diagonal only. Made entirely of plain squares and triangle patches, as here, the design emerges as a complex version of Bow Tie.

Indian Hatchet

The pattern shown here contains four identical double four-patch blocks, all based on squares and triangle patches. The plain stripe set in the patterned background has a strong diagonal line, with a point at each end of the "hatchet". This block would be effective with the stripes worked in different colors, provided that the background is consistent throughout.

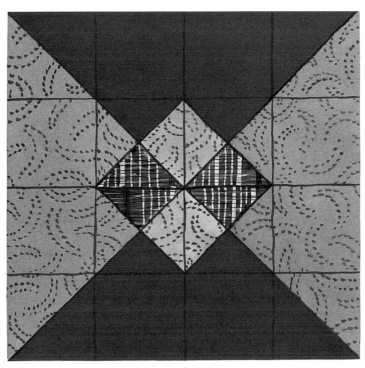

Granny's Choice

This double four-patch has a center "knot" that gives an effect similar to that of Bow Tie, but the construction is different. The four squares in the center are triangle patches arranged back to back so that the blue triangles form contrasting squares. It would be interesting to devise a quilt in which the two main fabrics stay the same, while the small contrasting squares in the center change in each block.

Octagon Patterns

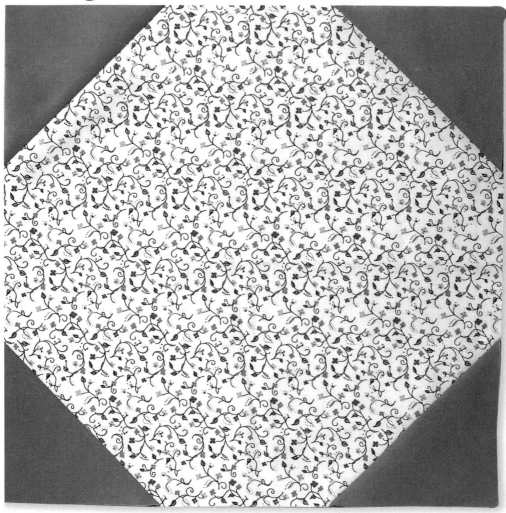

Octagon

This simple eight-sided geometric pattern uses squares of different sizes and is much easier to construct than the six-sided hexagon (see page 90). Also known as Snowball, it is made in a similar way to Bow Tie (see page 78), except that the small squares face out to the corners instead of into the center. Blocks can be placed side by side, creating small square motifs at regular intervals, but the octagon shape tends to get muddled unless the main fabric is alternated from block to block. The pattern looks very effective when alternated with plain unpieced blocks.

How to Construct an Octagon Block

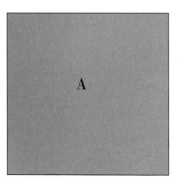

Cutting

Cut one large square from fabric A and four small squares from fabric B, each measuring one-third the size of the large square. Draw a diagonal line on the wrong side of each small square.

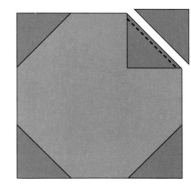

Adding the corners

Place a small square on each corner of the large square, right sides together. Stitch along the marked diagonal lines, trim away the excess triangles at each corner (see page 78) and press the seams toward the corner. While there is some waste in this method of construction, it means the bias seams remain stable while you work and are much less liable to stretch.

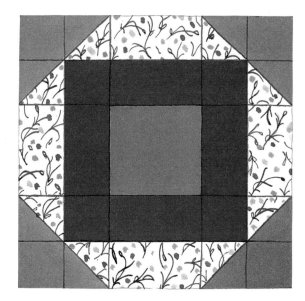

Kitchen Woodbox

Perhaps the shape resembles firewood stacked neatly in its box? At any rate, it makes a distinctive octagonal shape and is assembled from four identical nine-patch blocks (see page 34).

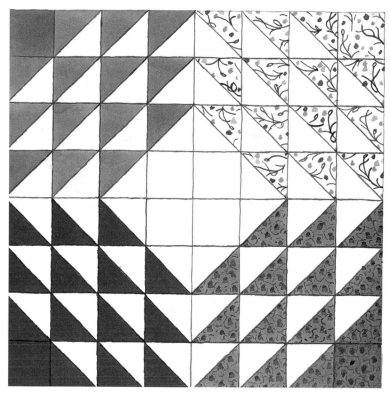

Ocean Wave

There are a number of variations of this pattern, but they all are composed of triangle patches of background and contrasting fabrics, with the contrasts pointing out toward the edge of the block. Here, each quadrant is a double four-patch (see page 57) made with a different contrasting fabric.

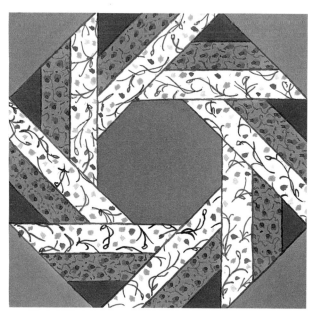

Basket Weave

This roly-poly octagon uses strip-pieced right-angled triangles (see page 44) to make a pattern around the eight-sided center. The corner triangles are cut from the same fabric and stitched on to square up the block.

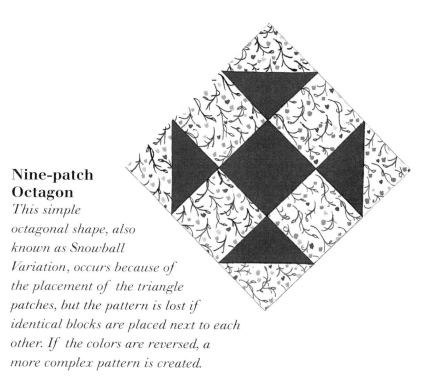

Nine-patch Octagon

This simple octagonal shape, also known as Snowball Variation, occurs because of the placement of the triangle patches, but the pattern is lost if identical blocks are placed next to each other. If the colors are reversed, a more complex pattern is created.

Sawtooth Patterns

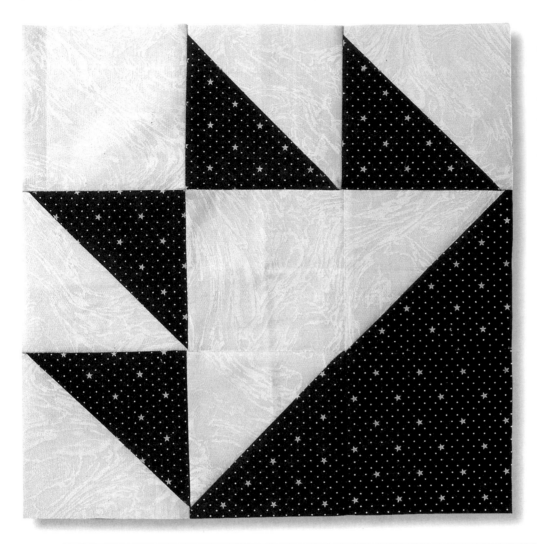

Sawtooth

The jagged edges of Sawtooth make it an aptly named block. Constructed here as a nine-patch, it can also be made with the larger triangles as single pieces of fabric. Sawtooth blocks can be combined to create geometric shapes outlined with "teeth" in a contrasting color. The teeth can point into the center or out toward the edges. The two larger triangles can be worked as a plain square that, when combined with more blocks, makes a large rectilinear area, again outlined with the points of the sawtooth.

How to Construct a Sawtooth Block

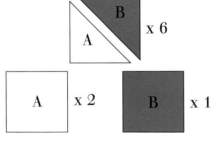

Cutting
Make six triangle squares using fabrics A and B (see pages 60 and 62). Cut two squares from fabric A and one from fabric B the same size as the finished pieced squares.

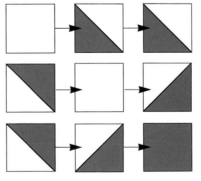

Making strips
Arrange the nine squares and stitch them into three rows, taking a ¹/4 in (5 mm) seam allowance. Press seams in opposite directions on each row.

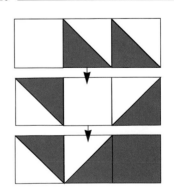

Joining rows
Join the assembled rows to make a nine-patch block (see page 34).

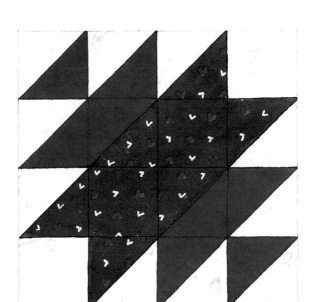

Mrs Taft's Choice

This pattern may or may not have been named after the wife of the 27th president of the United States, Helen "Nellie" Taft, who played a key role in her husband's term of office. It is a double four-patch (see page 57), made here in three colors to give a diagonal banner through the middle.

Old Star

This complex block can be constructed as a nine-patch, the four outer corners with their sawtoothed edges made in strips which are then attached to the large squares. It could be made using more than two colors, but its intricate design calls for individual blocks and sashing.

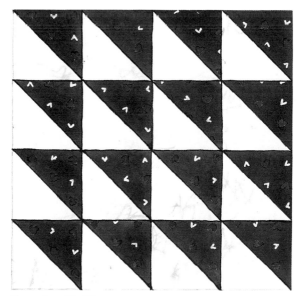

Sawtooth Rows

This simple double four-patch is made up of four identical rows in each direction, creating an overall pattern of triangles. The block makes good use of fabric scraps with a plain background, or you could try making each row — vertical, horizontal or diagonal — a different color.

Sawtooth Four-patch

Here, the four patches are themselves nine-patch blocks, again using only two colors. The dark background emphasizes the teeth in a way that would not happen if the colors used here were reversed.

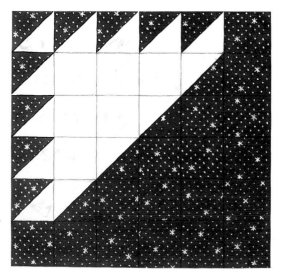

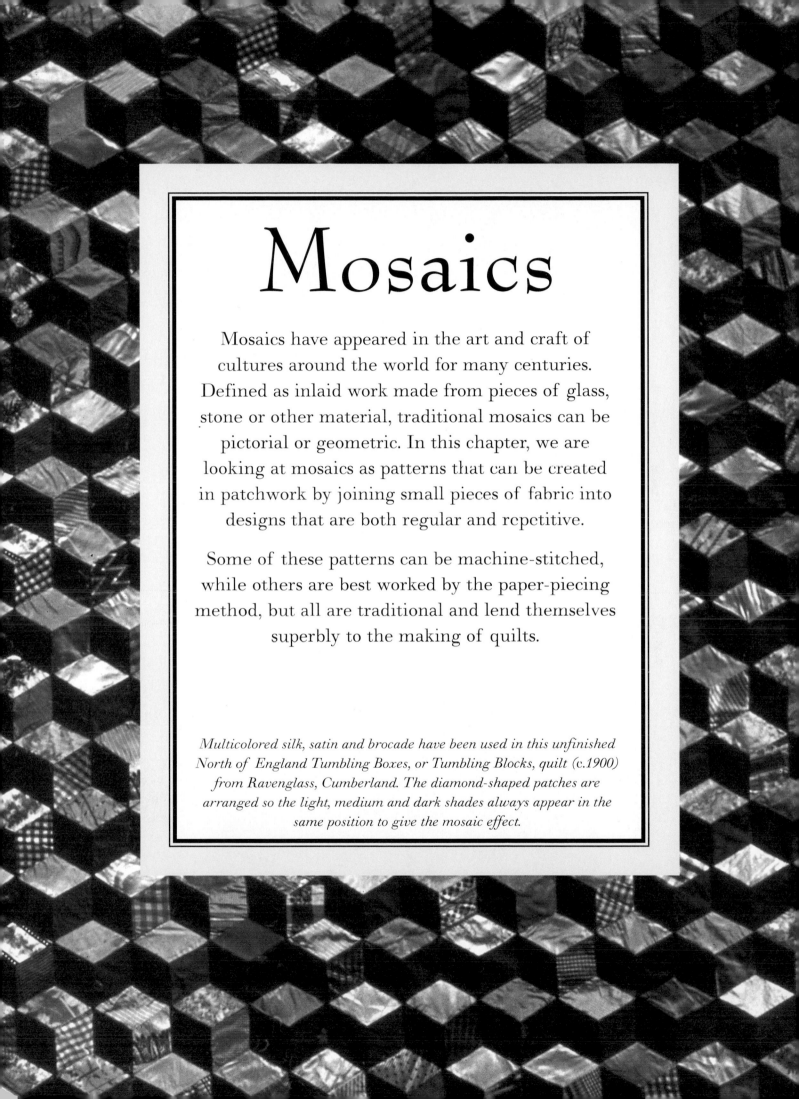

Mosaics

Mosaics have appeared in the art and craft of cultures around the world for many centuries. Defined as inlaid work made from pieces of glass, stone or other material, traditional mosaics can be pictorial or geometric. In this chapter, we are looking at mosaics as patterns that can be created in patchwork by joining small pieces of fabric into designs that are both regular and repetitive.

Some of these patterns can be machine-stitched, while others are best worked by the paper-piecing method, but all are traditional and lend themselves superbly to the making of quilts.

Multicolored silk, satin and brocade have been used in this unfinished North of England Tumbling Boxes, or Tumbling Blocks, quilt (c.1900) from Ravenglass, Cumberland. The diamond-shaped patches are arranged so the light, medium and dark shades always appear in the same position to give the mosaic effect.

Quilt Gallery

MOSAIC PATTERNS HAVE come to us mainly from the many surviving mosaics in the Mediterranean countries of Europe and North Africa. The Greeks of the ancient world were making mosaics before the birth of Chirst, and they passed on their techniques to the Romans, who were among the most skilled and prolific of mosaic makers. Roman mosaics can be found in all the areas which the empire colonized, and the technique was widely used in the Byzantine Empire. Islamic culture has given the world vast numbers of mosaics in the floors, walls and ceilings of mosques and other buildings, while the Mayans and the Aztecs made New World mosaics of great beauty. Many examples from all of these cultures survive, and their designs have been adapted to myriad other uses, for everything from floor and wall tiles to tabletops, from embroidery to patchwork and quilting patterns.

The ancient trade routes around the Mediterranean areas that are rich in mosaics point to a prolific interchange of design ideas. Mosaics in various cities such as Venice, home of some of the most beautiful examples in the world including the floors of St. Mark's cathedral, and Florence, as well as Naples and Pompeii, show clear regional variations, but many of the patterns are related to one another, perhaps because there are combinations of

Bordered Medallion Quilt

Made between 1837 and 1844, this quilt was worked by Ann Hutton-Wilson of Yarm, in the North of England, using a design created by her husband, Robert, who said she had "no eye for color". She was nevertheless a skilled needlewoman who assembled the seven separate pieced mosaic-pattern borders with the same precision as that with which she worked the double eight-pointed star in the center.

shapes that become obvious as a particular design is assembled. Islamic motifs found in mosaics throughout the Arabic world have an unequalled intricacy. Made in brilliant shades of tropical colors, many gleam with gold-colored pieces as well.

Some mosaics portray a scene or have a pictorial image in the center with geometric borders around the edge. They can be imitated on medallion quilts, on which the central square is surrounded by several borders of varying width, each different in color and design. Others simply display a pattern that repeats itself throughout the piece, sometimes using the same colors in each element of the design, but more often relying on the dark or light value of the colors to make the pattern.

MAKING MOSAIC PATTERNS

Drafting mosaic patterns can be done easily on isometric graph paper, which allows for the precise drawing of the angles in hexagons, diamonds and equilateral and isosceles triangles. Patterns involving squares, right-angled triangles, rectangles and octagons can be tried out on squared graph paper. It is a good idea to work out your ideas this way, using colored pencils to see the effect that is created when different colors are combined and juxtaposed in

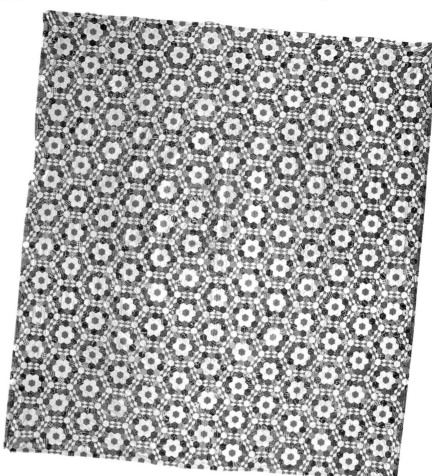

Hexagon

This Grandmother's Flower Garden variation (c.1860–70) was made by "an elderly countrywoman" from the Allenheads area of Northumberland, England. Worked in printed cottons in shades of pink, brown, blue and white, it is unfinished and still contains all the paper shapes used in the piecing, some dated 1841, others 1855. It has no backing and has not been quilted. The blue-and-white hexagons on the outer edges of each hexagonal block emphasize the honeycomb effect that this pattern creates.

various ways. (This is true of most designs, not just mosaic ones.)

The shapes used to create isometric patterns are usually best worked using the paper-piecing method, since it is so important for the angles to meet with precision. This tried-and-tested technique is more time-consuming than machine piecing, but provided you cut both your papers and the fabric carefully and correctly, it gives an accuracy that is difficult to match using a sewing machine. If you use isometric graph paper to cut the papers on which the patches are made, your precision will be enhanced.

THE SHAPES OF MOSAICS

The six-sided hexagon is among the most versatile of shapes, and hexagon quilts have been made by the traditional paper-piecing method since the 18th century. The colors can be highly organized or random, and there are beautiful examples of hexagon scrap quilts. Such quilts are almost always worked by hand — no one has yet found a way of strip-piecing hexagons! But hexagons can be used instead of squares to create secondary patterns, from the traditional Grandmother's Flower Garden through a hexagonal Ocean Wave to hexagon stars. In fact, many of the well-known patterns that use squares can be adapted to work as hexagon shapes.

The diamond is another favorite mosaic shape that lends itself to quilt design. Some of the patterns based on diamonds can be machine-stitched, but many are traditionally worked by the paper-piecing method to make the precise sharp points

Blazing Star

This patriotic American quilt from the late 19th century is worked in red, white and blue cottons. The central Blazing Star motif is 35 inches (90cm) square and is echoed at each corner by identical smaller blocks 11 inches (28cm) square which form the corners of the white inner border. The piece is thinly padded with diagonal quilting on the stars. The inner border between the small squares is quilted in the wineglass pattern, and the outer border, also white, is worked with a cable. The red binding creates a sharply defined edge.

that are essential to the effectiveness of the composition. Tumbling Blocks is but one of many patterns that are based on a diamond shape. Among others, there are a number of star patterns culminating in various spectacular Lone Star designs or Star of Bethlehem designs.

Both the Four-pointed Star and the Eight-pointed Star contain scope for countless variations, including the simple but beautiful Blazing Star through to Mariner's Compass in its most complex form. Many of the star patterns can be pieced by machine, or they can be worked by hand using the paper-piecing method. The most difficult aspect of most star patterns is the point in the center of the block, where between 4 and 64 seams meet. They should be joined precisely, and there are various techniques for achieving this feat, from pressing the seams open to making the block one section at a time.

Attic Windows is a pattern that creates beautiful three-dimensional mosaic effects by its arrangement of two strips of different colors mitered at one corner and bordering a large square "window". If this area is pieced in a geometric pattern, the possibilities for more intricate mosaic designs become even greater. Attic Windows, in its simplest form, is perhaps the easiest of the mosaic patterns that follow.

Star of Bethlehem

The neat piecing of this intricate eight-pointed star pattern, also called Lone Star, is matched by the beautifully executed quilting. Made in the 19th century in Bethlehem, Pennsylvania, it is a fine example of a mosaic pattern adapted to quiltmaking. The dark color used on each of the points on all the stars defines the tips precisely and links the centers to the points. The stars are outline quilted, with a shell pattern used as a filling on the white background. The inner border of Flying Geese surrounds three sides, presumably to mark the head end of the quilt, and the same fabrics have been used in the corner squares of the printed outer border. The top two corners are simple triangle patches, while the bottom two are small eight-pointed stars that echo the main design.

Hexagon Patterns

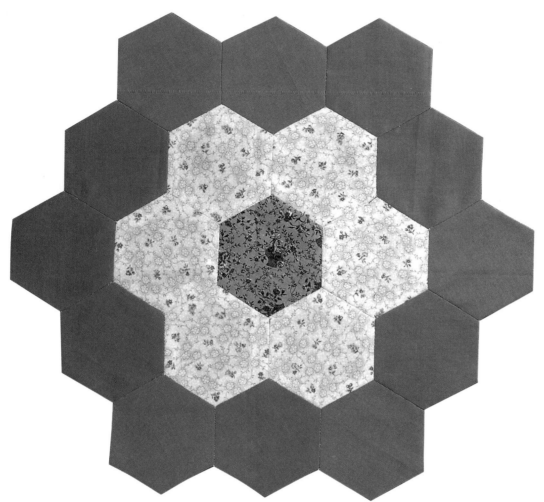

Grandmother's Flower Garden

The hexagon, one of the most basic geometric shapes, is usually worked using the English method (see page 14) over backing papers. Grandmother's Flower Garden, made up of two concentric rows of hexagons around a six-sided center, is one of the most popular of many variations; the second row can serve as the background separating single rows of "flowers". Leaving the papers in place until the piece is finished will help to stablilize the edges.

How to Construct a Grandmother's Flower Garden Block

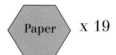 **Paper** x 19

 Fabric Fabric A x 1
Fabric B x 6
Fabric C x 12

Cutting
Use a template (see page 12) to cut 19 hexagons from paper. Use the "window" template with 1/4 in (5 mm) seam allowances to cut one hexagon from fabric A, six from fabric B and 12 from fabric C. Mark the seam allowances on the fabric shapes.

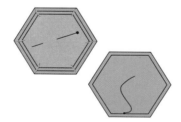

Making patches
Pin a paper shape to the wrong side of each fabric hexagon. Fold the seam allowance over the paper and baste in place, knotting the thread on the right side. This makes it easier to remove the papers later.

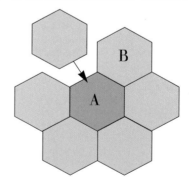

Stitching the block
Starting from the center, whipstitch the shapes together, first sewing one shape B to each side of the shape A and then working the side seams.

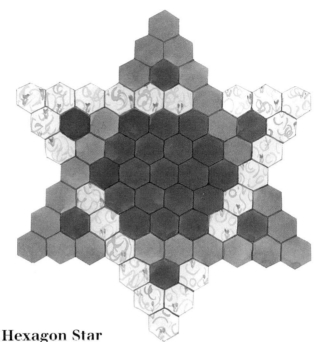

Hexagon Star

The versatility of the hexagon makes it useful for creating a myriad of secondary patterns such as this six-pointed star, composed entirely of six-sided figures. The placement of the colors creates further shapes in the two equilateral triangles that make up the star shape.

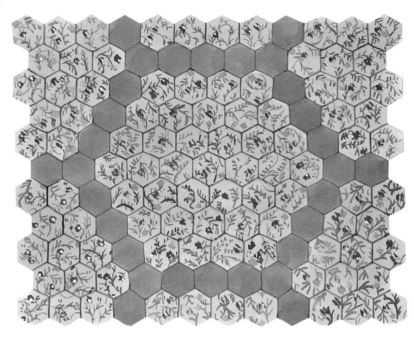

Tile Pattern

Here, hexagons have been joined in rows of the same color. These are broken occasionally by a shape of another color which, when they are strung together, forms the outline of a large hexagon. The variations are endless — look closely and you can see that the center of the tile could be worked in other colors to form a Grandmother's Flower Garden block.

Ocean Wave

The rise and fall of the waves is depicted in a number of patchwork patterns. This wave made from hexagons could go higher and lower if the rows of color are continued downward before you add shapes to push the line of color up again. It would make a beautiful, if time-consuming, pieced border (see page 19).

Diamond

Here, Grandmother's Flower Garden has been extended by one hexagon top and bottom, and extra rows of different colors are added. All the patterns shown here, and many more, can also be worked using the elongated six-sided shape known, somewhat morbidly, as the coffin.

Attic Window Patterns

Attic Window

The simplest form of this block consists of three fabrics – a main fabric, which is used for the center square, and two contrasting fabrics, which are set along two sides. The "window" can be a pieced block; the "frame" pieces can be cut straight and mitered at the corner, but the construction shown here looks the same and makes an easy and effective pattern. All the variations shown opposite are called by the name Attic Window, but they are more complicated to put together.

How to Construct an Attic Window Block

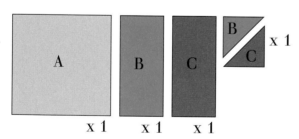

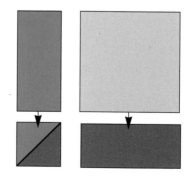

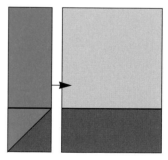

Cutting

Cut one large square from the main fabric A. Cut one small square from fabrics B and C, and one strip the same width as the small squares from B and C. Cut the small squares once on the diagonal (you will need only one of the resulting triangles in each fabric).

Joining the pieces

Stitch the triangles together along the bias edge to form a triangle patch (see page 60), then stitch strip B to the fabric B edge of the triangle patch. Stitch strip C to one edge of the fabric A square.

Making the block

Matching seams carefully, stitch the two units together as shown to form a block.

Pieced Attic Window

This nine-patch block (see page 34) is different in its construction from its cousin opposite, graphically illustrating the fact that diverse patterns sometimes end up with the same name. Made simply from squares and triangle patches, it has a center square that makes its "window", which peeps out onto the world from under the slant of the "eaves".

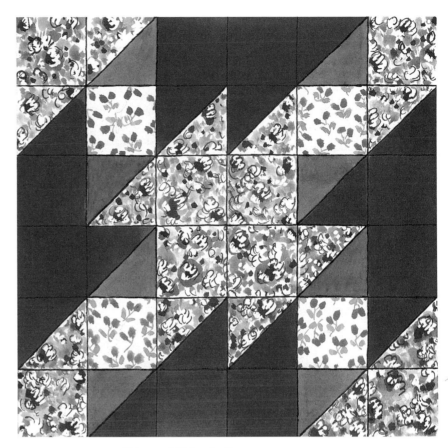

Pieced Block I

Here, four pieced Attic Window blocks, similar to the single one on the left, have been combined with the center made from patterned squares to give a pattern that has moved further away from the idea of an upstairs window.

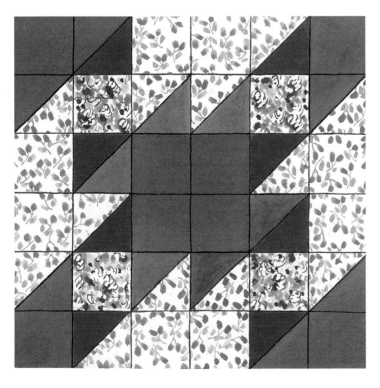

Pieced Block II

In this double nine-patch, two blocks identical to the single one above, have been combined with two more in which two of the fabrics have been reversed. The plain corner squares in all four units remain the same patches and meet in the middle. The block, a negative image of Pieced Block I, is still no closer to conveying the image of an attic window. It is, however, an attractive and interesting design for a quilt.

Tumbling Block Patterns

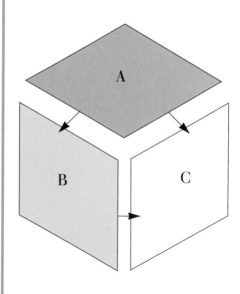

Tumbling Blocks

Also known as Baby Blocks, this charming pattern is highly versatile and works as well in sophisticated silks and velvets as it does in baby-print cottons to create a highly effective, three-dimensional feel. The secret of its success lies in choosing strong color contrasts – light, medium and dark values – and in careful piecing at the corners. It is usually constructed using the "English", or paper-piecing, method (see page 14), which makes it easier to join the corner points neatly. Extremely attractive shading can be produced across a quilt by the careful use of color.

How to Construct a Tumbling Blocks Block

Cutting and stitching a unit

Make a template (see page 12) for the diamond shape and use it to cut out paper backing diamonds (finished size), and fabric shapes in the three colors with seam allowances added. Baste each fabric shape to a backing paper, then whipstitch one shape of each color together to make a unit.

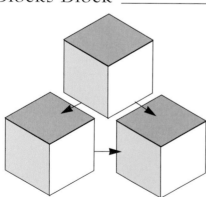

Joining units

Combine the desired number of units by whipstitching along the edges. The backing papers allow the pieces, which have bias edges, to keep their shape, so do not remove them until the finished quilt is complete.

Inner City Block

This stacked block consists of a Tumbling Block that has been extended by adding diamonds at the sides and bottom to make a Y shape. The colors of the added shapes must match those of the Tumbling Block, so you need three diamonds, each a different color, for the basic block and an additional two of each color – six extra in total – for the base and arms.

Inner City Pattern

When Inner City blocks are combined, the origin of the name of the block is apparent. Its look of a crowded cityscape, with a skyline of tall buildings, makes this a block to use pictorially, with shading for earth and sky offsetting the mass of the houses and streets.

Block Puzzle

This block can be seen as three Tumbling Blocks with corner diamonds creating a hexagon, or as a six-point star with fill-in diamonds between each point. No matter how it is perceived, it is still constructed from the same diamond shapes and worked by the paper-piecing method. Note that whichever way you turn it, it still creates the illusion of three-dimensional blocks. These blocks can be combined as ordinary hexagons (see pages 90–91) into larger pieces or used as individual motifs.

Four-pointed Star Patterns

Four-pointed Star

Star patterns come in many shapes, from four-pointed versions as here, to the 32 or more points found in some Mariner's Compass designs. Most require templates and can be made using the English method (see page 14). However, since they usually have straight seams, many can also be pieced by machine. This version, known as Blazing Star or Mother's Delight, can be simplified by making the corner points in only one fabric, or by eliminating them completely. The major problem with all star patterns is joining the units neatly in the center of the block.

How to Construct a Blazing Star Block

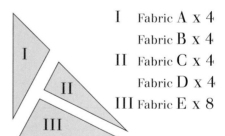

I   Fabric A x 4
    Fabric B x 4
II Fabric C x 4
    Fabric D x 4
III Fabric E x 8

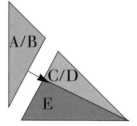

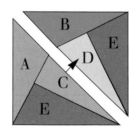

Cutting

Make templates for the three shapes that make up the block (see page 12). Then cut fabrics as follows: shape 1 – cut 4 x fabric A and 4 x fabric B; shape II – cut 4 x fabric C and 4 x fabric D; shape III – cut 8 x fabric E.

Making the units

Taking a ¹/4 in (5 mm) seam, join a shape II and a shape III and press the seams to one side. Then stitch a shape I to the seamed edge. Repeat to make eight units, referring carefully to the photograph to check the color sequence.

Making the patches

Join alternate units to make four identical square patches. Join the squares as a four-patch block (see page 56), matching the seams in the center carefully.

Laced Star

This complicated-looking variation has its four-point origins almost hidden by the long diagonal points that give a pinwheel feel to the block. It is constructed from four basic shapes, two of which are background, with the remaining two cut in the same color for each section, creating a woven effect.

Combined Blazing Star

When Blazing Star blocks are combined, a secondary pattern emerges — as happens with most patchwork patterns. Here, the corner points meet in the center of the double four-patch and create a curved shape. As more and more blocks are added, the number of these rounded areas increases and, depending on the colors used, becomes more prominent.

Barbara Bannister Star

This version contains only four shapes and is constructed in a similar way to Blazing Star. The square on point shown in checked fabric can be emphasized by making the inner triangles lighter or by matching them to the background fabric. This version creates stunning secondary patterns when blocks are combined.

North Star

The construction of this variation, based on four shapes, is also similar to Blazing Star. If the two central shapes are made from the same fabric, the star becomes more definite, while matching the small center triangles to the background fabric, as here, makes the star seem to twinkle.

Eight-pointed Star Patterns

Eight-pointed Star

The eight-pointed star is one of the most enduring of all patchwork motifs. Seen here in its simplest form, made from eight diamonds in two alternating colors, it provides the basis for numerous quilts. These include the intricate and beautiful Lone Star patterns, in which concentric bands of diamonds radiate out into the final eight points. Because there are so many seams overlapping at the center, it can be tricky to keep the points sharp in the middle, but pressing all the seams open can make the task easier.

How to Construct an Eight-pointed Star Block

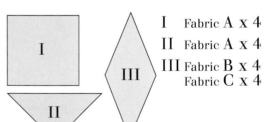

I Fabric **A** x 4
II Fabric **A** x 4
III Fabric **B** x 4
    Fabric **C** x 4

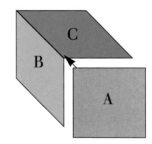

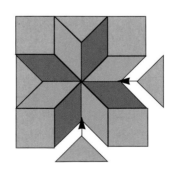

Cutting

Make templates for the diamond and triangle shapes (see page 12). Cut four corner squares and four triangles from background fabric, and four diamonds from fabrics A and B, adding $^1/4$ in (5 mm) seam allowances to all pieces.

Making the patches

Taking a $^1/4$ in (5 mm) seam, stitch a fabric B diamond to a C diamond and repeat to make four pairs. Add a corner square to each unit, stitching from the corner out in each direction. Join the units into pairs, then join the pairs together to make a star, matching seams carefully.

Assembling the block

Add triangles in the points to finish the block, stitching from the point of the triangle out in each direction.

LeMoyne Star

Tradition has it that this early star pattern was named after the LeMoyne brothers Pierre and Jean-Baptiste, early residents of New Orleans, and that as the design travelled north the name became corrupted into Lemon Star. With its divided points in alternating colors, it was a highly popular pattern in the early 1900s.

Virginia Star

This is a simplified version of the Lone Star, or Star of Bethlehem, in which the center is an eight-pointed star and concentric rings of the same diamond shape are added As the bands of color are applied, the design becomes more and more complex.

Carpenter's Wheel

Also known as Broken Star, this popular pattern combines squares with diamonds to create two different shapes of star surrounded by a ring of color. It looks stunning worked in just two colors, and becomes three-dimensional when colors are alternated in the outer ring, as here.

Lily

Here, a simple eight-pointed star has been transformed into an organic shape by the use of a different color in one quadrant. The points of the flower head in the other three sections are set apart, and the addition of a stem strip adds to the feeling of a bloom.

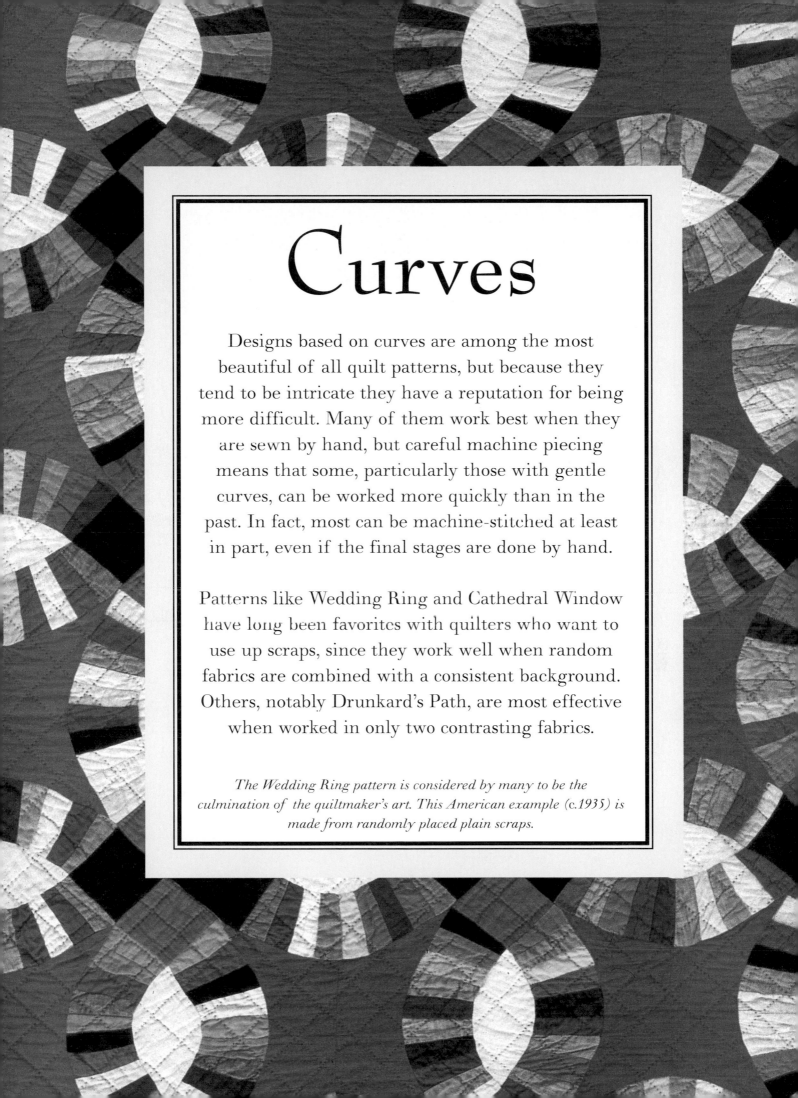

Curves

Designs based on curves are among the most beautiful of all quilt patterns, but because they tend to be intricate they have a reputation for being more difficult. Many of them work best when they are sewn by hand, but careful machine piecing means that some, particularly those with gentle curves, can be worked more quickly than in the past. In fact, most can be machine-stitched at least in part, even if the final stages are done by hand.

Patterns like Wedding Ring and Cathedral Window have long been favorites with quilters who want to use up scraps, since they work well when random fabrics are combined with a consistent background. Others, notably Drunkard's Path, are most effective when worked in only two contrasting fabrics.

The Wedding Ring pattern is considered by many to be the culmination of the quiltmaker's art. This American example (c.1935) is made from randomly placed plain scraps.

Quilt Gallery

LTHOUGH CURVES must be joined with great care, the resulting patterns have a sinuous vitality that is impossible to achieve using straight-sided shapes. Perhaps the most familiar of curved patterns is Wedding Ring, or Double Wedding Ring, with its interlocking circles that symbolize the marriage bonds. The scraps traditionally used to make the rings themselves may represent the variety – and vagaries – of married life. The pattern appeared in the early 1900s and seems to have reached the height of its popularity during the Depression years, when piecing from scraps was a way of spending less. It can be bordered in several ways. The quilt on the previous pages has the rings set on a narrow squared-off black background, with a wider blue border that echoes the blue background. Others have a single border, while many are backed and bound by following the shape of the outside rings to make a curved edge all around. There are a number of variations, and of patterns with bridal names. Bear in mind that this is not a quilt for the beginner.

Cathedral Window, sometimes known as Mayflower, is included in this chapter because the final shape of the pattern is curved, although the pieces are cut as straight-sided squares. This is another

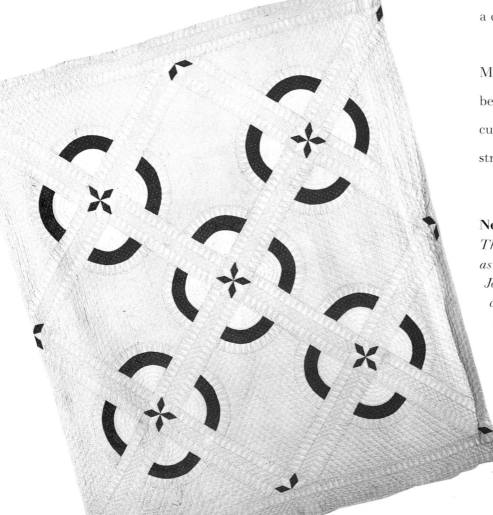

New York Beauty
This seemingly simple pattern, also known as Crown of Thorns, is similar to Josephine's Knot. Made in the early 20th century, the quilt is highly intricate, with small yellow triangles pieced with the white background to form the straight diagonal strips and the outlines around the red circles. A diagonal grid of quilting has been worked in the open spaces, with outline quilting around the pattern.

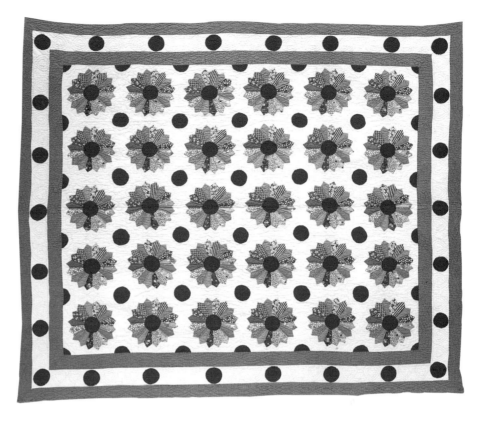

Depression-era favorite, probably because it used scraps for the "glass" in the "windows", which gave these quilts the look of stained glass in a church window. This is a bedcover without batting, and the backing is also the foundation fabric, making it an integral part of the design. It is heavy and should be treated carefully to make sure the stitching does not come apart when the piece is handled and cleaned.

If the method for assembling Cathedral Window is reversed, the resulting pattern is known as Secret Garden, where the curved shapes become the petals of flowers instead of stained-glass windows.

FANS AND PLATES

A number of popular patterns belong to a family of fan- and plate-shaped designs.

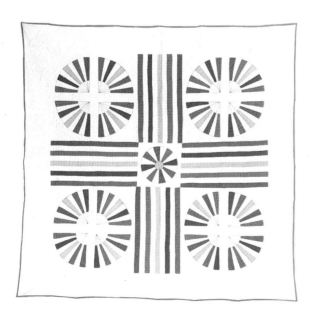

There are countless variations on the basic theme, in which the outer points take on a wide range of shapes from flat to pointed. All work extremely well made from scraps of material, and because of this, and the fact that the designs echo the shapes popular in the Art Deco period, they are also associated with the 1930s. Many beautiful examples survive that were made from the printed cotton fabrics used to hold

Noughts and Crosses
Curves lend themselves to unusual treatments, such as this American quilt from c.1935. The pastel color palette, the straight cross in the middle made from strips, and the variation of the Dresden Plate used for the circular corner motifs all combine to bring a vibrant optical movement to this interesting piece.

Dresden Plate
An uncommonly high number of printed fabrics have been used to make the pointed segments of this Ohio Amish Dresden Plate pattern. Dating from 1910–20, it contains a number of other elements that set it apart. The red circles in the center of each plate are repeated in the background spaces between each block and are echoed in the wide middle border to give a playful feel to this beautiful piece.

Robbing Peter to Pay Paul

A highly traditional treatment of a curved pattern has been worked here by Tom Cuff, an American quilt artist, who has arranged his patches into a precise series of positive/negative blocks. Had he assembled the blocks in a different way, he would have created a different pattern, such as Drunkard's Path or Falling Timbers.

feed for chickens and other animals, as well as commodities such as flour and sugar. The patterns, especially the Fan, have been used for much longer, however, and beautiful Victorian examples made from luxurious silks and velvets can be seen on display in quilt museums.

The straight seams joining the fan blades or the plate segments can, of course, be stitched by machine, or they can be worked using the "English" or paper-piecing method. The edges are usually joined by hand to the background, which can be cut

to the necessary shape or made as a square block on which the fan or plate can be mounted. This method of applying the pattern to the background gives a stronger quilt, but leaves a double layer of fabric to be quilted.

Fan blocks are particularly versatile and look effective when set in regimented rows with the blades all pointing in the same direction, on point so the fans stand upright, with points meeting, or with blocks alternating in rows that snake in sinuous curves diagonally across the quilt.

Outline or echo quilting is widely used on traditional examples, and quilting a motif in the space left by the background on a fan block is also highly effective.

TWO-COLOR PATTERNS

One of the most appealing aspects of the designs that rely on alternating light and dark colors are their names: Drunkard's Path (known as Solomon's Puzzle or Old Maid's Puzzle in the teetotal Amish tradition), Robbing Peter to Pay Paul, Rocky Road to California, Orange Peel, Falling Timbers, Melon Patch, Dolly Madison's Workbox, Pumpkin Vine. While these patterns can be worked in several colors, they tend to be more effective when only two – highly contrasting – shades are used. If the curve is fairly gentle, the patches can be stitched carefully by machine, but hand piecing is a more traditional method. Paper piecing can be used, but it is an unnecessary step if the stitching lines are marked carefully on the fabric. The pattern is achieved by taking a curved segment from one corner of a square and replacing it with an identical section of the second color. When an equal number of positive/negative and negative/positive patches have been worked, they are assembled into the arrangement that gives the desired pattern.

The straight seams can be machine-stitched if you wish, but make sure the corners are matched precisely. Several of the setting variations, which are the factors that determine the name of the pattern in most cases, leave blank spaces that can be filled with single quilting motifs.

The most difficult of all the curved patterns is probably Clamshell, which relies on absolute precision in both cutting and piecing, but it is a highly effective pattern that can repay the effort involved. It is not a quilt for the beginner, but you could practice it on a smaller piece such as a cushion cover.

Drunkard's Path
Dated 1886, this piece is called Robbing Peter to Pay Paul in the catalog of the American Museum in Britain, but the setting is more often known as Drunkard's Path. Perhaps the tactful name was used because the quilt was made as a gift for Mrs Patty (Armour) Washburn by ladies from the Congregational Church in Oriskany Falls, New York.

Clamshell Patterns

Basic Clamshell

Clamshell is one of the old traditional patterns based on natural forms. Its simple rounded elegance make it an attractive choice for a quilt, but its somewhat complicated construction, using the English method (see page 14), has limited its appeal to modern quilters. It can be used to make a pieced border, or the clamshell effect can be recreated by a scalloped edge. Since the curve is perfectly circular, it is straightforward to create a template by drawing around a glass and adding the stem.

How to Construct a Clamshell Block

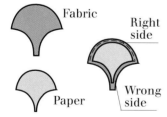

Cutting

Cut templates from paper (see page 12). Cut patches from fabric, adding seam allowances all around. Pin a fabric shape to each paper, then fold the seam allowance around the top edge over the paper and baste in place. Mark the top center.

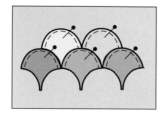

Arranging the design

On a piece of cork board or heavy card, draw a straight row of curves, using the paper template as a pattern. Pin a row of patches in place, then add a second row, arranging the colors as you wish.

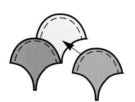

Stitching the patches

Slipstitch the first patch from the bottom row to the first patch from the top row. Begin at the marked point on the lower patch and sew along the seamline of the bottom curve of the upper patch.

Making the block

Add the next patch from the bottom row in the same way, and repeat the sequence to make rows of the desired length. Trim the edges, if necessary, to make a block.

Shell Patchwork

A number of intricate designs can be made using the basic Clamshell patch. Here, the stems point toward each other, and curved tops fill in the gaps created on either side. Using the same background in alternating rows, with different fabrics filling the spaces in between, makes an interesting mosaic.

Double Axehead

In this aptly named pattern, the rounded top curve of the shape stops higher than on the Clamshell and is repeated on the opposite edge at the bottom, with a "bite" taken out of each side. The template can be made by drawing a circle of the desired size and marking intersecting circles on each side to create the narrow waist of the shape.

Shells

The basic Clamshell pattern can be worked to great effect in bands of repeating color. Here, the rows run horizontally, but the pattern also looks stunning worked in diagonal bands. Note that the template used here allows the shells to be positioned so that there is a sharp point at the bottom of each patch.

Fan Patterns

Fan

Often called Grandmother's Fan, this popular pattern has dozens of variations. The fan is a traditional design that occurs in motifs from all over the world, and it is used as a quilting pattern (page 140) as well as in patchwork and appliqué. Based on a quarter-circle, this design can be altered to incorporate more or fewer blades with flat, curved or pointed ends, and provides a good way to use up scraps of fabric.

How to Construct a Fan Block

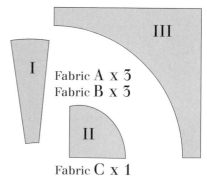

Fabric A x 3
Fabric B x 3

Fabric C x 1

Fabric D x 1

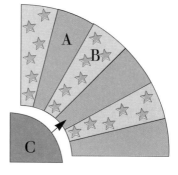

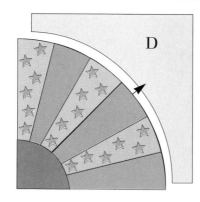

Cutting
Make templates for the blades, background and small corner pieces (see page 12), and cut out all the pieces. Remember that the colors of the blades should alternate for best effect.

Making the fan
Taking a ¹/4 in (5 mm) seam, sew the blades together along the straight edges and press the seams. Add the small corner piece carefully to avoid stretching the curve.

Adding the background
Pin the background piece in place and stitch carefully by hand or machine (see page 16). The background fabric should lie perfectly flat.

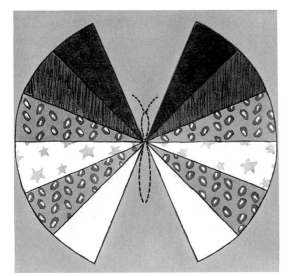

Butterfly

This realistic variation is often worked in appliqué, but can be made in patchwork as well. The wings can be divided into more or fewer sections, and the butterfly's body can be embroidered in outline, as here, or made in appliqué.

Snake in the Hollow

While fans are usually set all in the same direction, many quilts have alternating blocks that give diagonal bands of color. What makes Snake in the Hollow different is its double fans, each of which joins its neighbor to create an intriguing sinuous curve that shows how this pattern got its name.

Simple Dresden Plate

The simplest form of Dresden Plate uses large segments and only two colors, but this pattern is highly effective as a scrap pattern, too. The center circle can be stitched in or appliquéd to cover the bottom edges of the segments.

Dresden Plate

This traditional pattern has been popular for decades, but its heyday was probably in the 1920s and '30s, when it was often made using flour sacks and incorporating Art Deco shapes into its variations.

Drunkard's Path Patterns

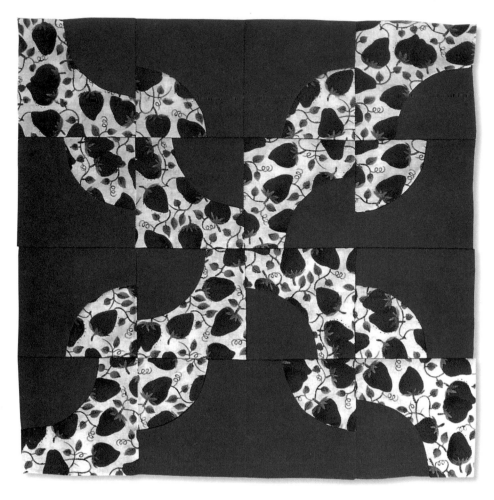

Drunkard's Path

This four-patch block uses curved seams to make a pattern reminiscent of an inebriate staggering home after a jolly night out. The pattern was used in the 19th century to make "cause" quilts; designs in blue and white are thought to have been made in support of the temperance movement of the day. *Below:* Combining several blocks increases the complexity.

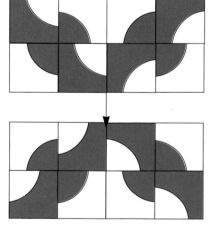

How to Construct a Drunkard's Path Block

I   Fabric A x 8
    Fabric B x 8
II Fabric A x 8
    Fabric B x 8

Cutting and piecing
Cut eight sections of each piece in fabric A and fabric B. Join the small fabric A pieces to the large fabric B pieces, and vice versa. Clip into the seam allowance before pressing, to encourage seams to lie flat.

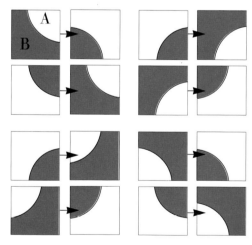

Joining pairs
Combine the pieced squares into pairs, alternating lights and darks. Then join two pairs together, again alternating colors as shown, to make four patches.

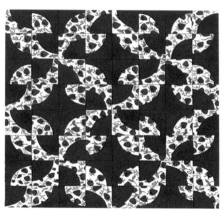

Making the block
Matching seams carefully, combine the four-patch units into a block (see How to Construct a Four-patch Block, page 56).

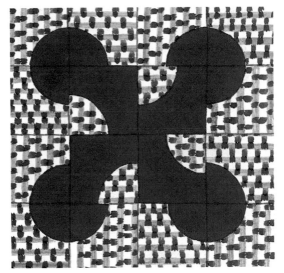

Wonder of the World I

This variation uses curved-seam squares arranged in a spiralling windmill shape that appears to be mounted on a background. There are 12 light/dark squares and four dark/light ones.

Falling Timbers

Constructed from the same elements as Drunkard's Path – eight each of two curved shapes – Falling Timbers is reminiscent of trees falling in a wood. The squares are joined alternately according to color. If the lights and darks are swapped and the squares turned 90 degrees, the resulting pattern is known as Vine of Friendship.

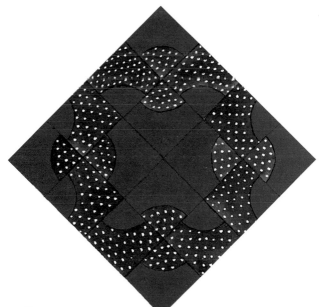

Dove

This elegant variation again uses eight squares in a configuration of light/dark and eight dark/light, but arranges them to give a central motif with two types of corner in a matching fabric. Combining several such blocks creates an interesting meandering "patch" through the background.

Wonder of the World II

This double four-patch variation consists of two "windmill" units containing eight light/ dark squares and two cross-shaped units containing eight dark/ light squares to give a spiral effect.

Wedding Ring Patterns

Wedding Ring

Also known as Double Wedding Ring, this is an enduring pattern in spite of its complex construction. Evidence shows that it is a 20th-century creation that was at the peak of its popularity in the 1920s and '30s, so it most likely owes some of its fame to the fact that it relied heavily on scraps during the Great Depression. It remains a favorite challenge for the more experienced quilter. There are a number of patterns available to purchase or trace from a book. The fabrics for this block have been chosen at random, while the ones below have been standardized to simplify the instructions.

How to Construct a Wedding Ring Block

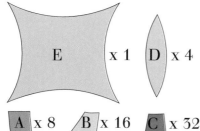

E x 1   D x 4

A x 8   B x 16   C x 32

Cutting and making strips

Make templates for all shapes and cut out fabric pieces (see page 12). Join four C shapes together, then add one B shape to each end of the strip. Repeat to make eight curved strips.

D

Joining strips

Stitch one strip to one edge of a D shape. Repeat to make four units. Add a square A shape to each end of each of the remaining four strips.

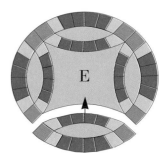

E

Making the block

Stitch the curved unit containing shape D to the longer stitched strip. Repeat to make four units. Stitch one pieced unit to each curved side of the center piece E.

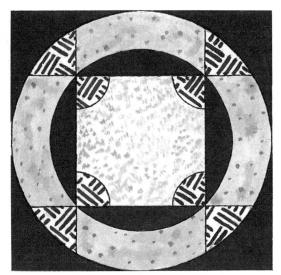

Queen's Crown

The curved pieces in this pattern are joined together into a ring and then joined to the inner unit, with the outside corners added last. The longer parts of the ring could be made from pieced units in the same way as Wedding Ring.

Crossroads

This block has its curves in the corners, while the pieced chains make the diagonal "crossroad" sections. When several blocks are joined together, the curves create rings and the crossroads become longer. Accurate cutting and piecing are essential.

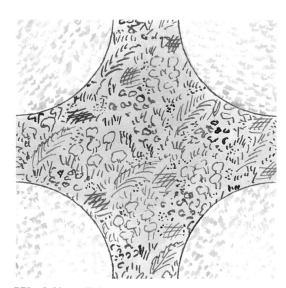

Wedding Ring

This simple curved pattern is not so much a variation of the basic Wedding Ring as a different block with the same name, which owes its construction more to Drunkard's Path (see page 110). When several blocks are combined, the curved corners become the "rings" – the resulting quilt would made an elegant marriage gift.

Boston Puzzle

This pattern is related to the Wedding Ring on the left, but the curves appear as "bites" taken out of each side. When blocks are combined, the semicircular bites become full circles that create a polka-dot pattern that works very well when scraps are matched on each side.

Josephine's Knot Patterns

Josephine's Knot

Perhaps this block was named after Napoleon's empress? Or maybe it was named after the otherwise unknown Josephine who designed it? In any case it is a simple and elegant pattern using curved shapes, with the "ribbons" crossing in the middle giving a knotted effect. It is a good block for a sampler quilt, and when it is combined with more of the same, it creates outlined squares.

How to Construct a Josephine's Knot Block

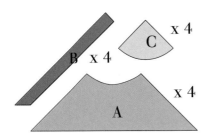

Cutting

To make templates, divide a square of the finished size diagonally into four triangles. For the rectangular strip, remove the left-hand edge of one triangle. Cut out the cone shape from the triangle's apex. Cut four fabric patches for each shape, adding ¹/4 in (5 mm) seam allowances.

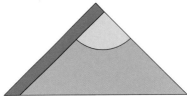

Making the units

Stitch the curved seams to join each piece C to a piece A. Then stitch one long strip B to the left-hand edge of each pieced triangle.

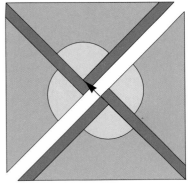

Making the block

Stitch the pieced triangles together in pairs. Matching the center seams, stitch along the long edges to complete the block.

Compass

This complicated-looking block is actually a four-patch in which each unit contains only three basic shapes. Each square is divided by straight lines running from the corner to the center of adjacent sides. The top of the central resulting diamond shape is then rounded off to make an ice-cream cone shape. Making a quilt in just two fabrics gives a lively harlequin effect, provided that the corners of the squares are matched carefully.

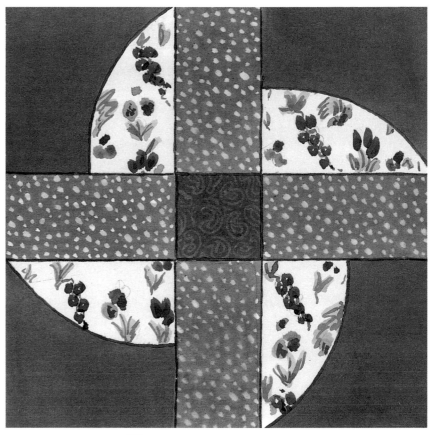

Nocturne

Here, the curves sweep from one corner to the midpoint on the adjacent side of a square. The four square patches are divided by straight strips that meet at a smaller square in the center. The construction is the same as a nine-patch block (see page 34).

Turtle

This jolly block owes some of its construction to Drunkard's Path (see page 110), with the straight head and tail added in diagonal corners using templates. The four-patch form (see page 56) makes it an easy block to construct, but the individual blocks need to be sashed if the shape of the turtle is to be maintained. It makes a nice block in a sampler quilt for a child.

Cathedral Window Patterns

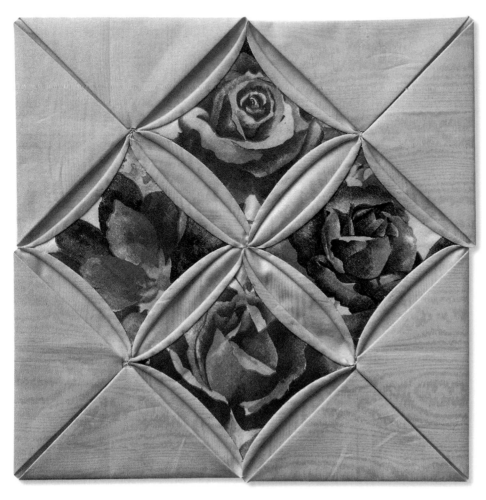

Cathedral Window

Cathedral Window, also known as Mayflower patchwork, is a technique that involves folding squares of background fabric, then stitching the resulting squares together and inserting contrasting fabric, which is caught in place under the folded edges of the background. This results in the look of a stained-glass church window. These pieces need no batting, and the backing is built in to the assembly of the block, so the quilt is lightweight and makes an attractive bedspread. Contrary to the myth that Pilgrim women made such bedcovers on board the *Mayflower*, evidence suggests that this is a modern method that was at the peak of its popularity during the 1920s and '30s.

How to Construct a Cathedral Window Block

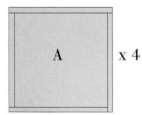

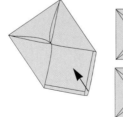

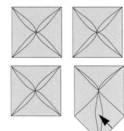

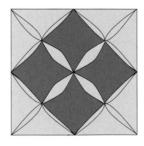

Cutting

Cut out four large A squares and four small B squares – the large ones are twice the size of the small ones. On the large squares, turn under $1/8$ in (3 mm) all around and press.

Folding the large squares

Fold all four corners of each large background square into the center and baste to hold them in place. Repeat to reduce the squares to half their original size. Slipstitch the four folded squares together in pairs.

Making the block

Pin a small B square over the joining seams as shown. Roll back the folded edges on each side of each small square and slipstitch them in place to enclose the raw edges of the small squares.

Orange Peel

Although this pattern resembles Cathedral Window in appearance, it is a seamed block put together with curved seams. It is not constructed with folded squares, but by cutting templates with seam allowances added and stitching carefully along the curves to make the units for a four-patch block (see page 56).

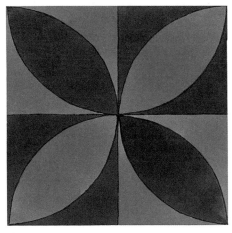

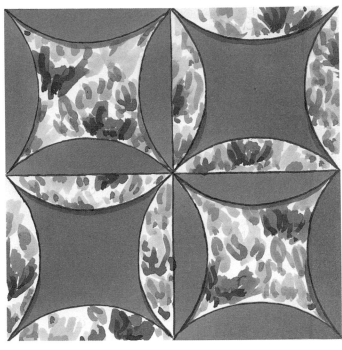

Alabama Star Beauty

This block is a straightforward variation of Orange Peel, with a third color and a four-pointed star added. However, it needs to be pieced carefully in four identical, but not square, units that can then be joined in pairs.

Japanese Folded Squares

This method incorporates batting in its construction to make the quilt warmer. Background circles are cut and a fold pressed to the wrong side, then a square of batting covered by contrasting fabric is centered on each one, wrong sides together. The turned-under edges of the circles are folded over the contrasting squares and slipstitched in place.

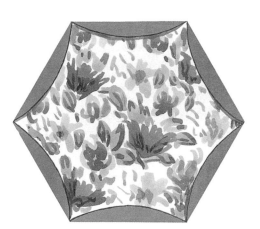

Secret Garden

This folded patchwork pattern is the reverse of Cathedral Window. The four background squares are folded once as shown in the construction method (see left), and the contrasting fabric is basted in the center of each square before the second fold is made. When the corners have been basted after the second fold, the folded edges are rolled back and slipstitched in place.

Japanese Folded Hexagon

This is made in the same way as the Square pattern above, except that the background circle is divided into six parts and the center fabric and batting are cut to a hexagon shape. The padded hexagons can be assembled into any of the blocks on page 91.

Quilting Patterns

Ultimately, the thing that makes a quilt is the quilting. The stitches that hold the layers of a quilt together – the quilting – can be large or small, even or uneven. They can be randomly placed, but carefully planned and worked, they enhance a piece of fabric, pieced or plain, in a unique way.

The patterns that follow range from traditional designs, such as wreaths, feathers, cables and baskets, to more modern abstract motifs and simple shapes that can be used for outline quilting. Many designs can be adapted for Italian, or corded, quilting, or for trapunto or sashiko (see page 25).

Peach sateen was beautifully and expertly quilted in the tradition of the North-east of England in 1935 by Mrs M.E. Shepherd as a wedding quilt for her son. Because he never married, the quilt was never used.

Quilt Gallery

QUILTING HAS PROBABLY been used on fabric since humans learned to clothe themselves. Certainly there is historical evidence of quilted garments from as far afield as ancient China and ancient Egypt, and fragments of quilted cloth still exist from the Middle Ages. The word quilt was used in various forms before the 13th century and could describe quilted bedcovers as well as quilted items of clothing. Quilted armor was worn by medieval soldiers under their chain mail for warmth, comfort and protection, and women in most areas of Europe wore quilted petticoats.

Fine quilted clothing was extremely fashionable in 17th- and 18th-century Europe, and the skills needed to produce it were widely known and practiced. The early colonists who sailed across the Atlantic to escape poverty and persecution took their knowledge of stitching, and their frugal habits, with them to the Americas. Here, no doubt, both practices helped many to survive the harsh climate and privations of life in an alien land. By the 19th century the skills involved in quilting were being applied to decorative bedcovers on both sides of the Atlantic, and three of the quilting traditions that are most admired today reached their heights. From the early 1800s, women and men in the north of England, centered in the north-eastern counties of Durham and Northumberland,

Split Bars

This beautifully quilted Amish piece (c.1910) illustrates most of the characteristics of its tradition. The plain, sober colors have been arranged into an elegant version of the Split Bars pattern with a wide border. The quilting moves from a central eight-point star, enclosed by feathered circles, to a crosshatched grid across the bars themselves. The grapevine on the inner border has been spaced precisely to loop into each corner, while the bunches of grapes hang above and below each of the yellow bars. On the outer border, the traditional baskets sit with their bases firmly on the outside edge, while the ones in the corners are turned on point.

Reversible Quilt

This elegant sateen quilt with its preprinted border (c.1910) was made by Mrs Stewart from Bowburn, County Durham, a widow who was a professional quilter. She ran one of the quilting clubs in the area that allowed purchasers to pay a small sum – in this case, one shilling – over a certain number of weeks (in this case, twenty) giving the buyer time to earn the money while the quilter made the quilt, an early version of the layaway plan.

were engaged in quilting as a livelihood, participating in a cottage industry that kept their skills alive until the late 20th century when their importance and artistic value were generally recognized.

In Wales, meanwhile, a similar skill bank had grown up in another poor area of rural Britain. Welsh quilting was done mainly on wool fabrics, with a consequent increase in the size of the stitches, and the patterns were more geometric than those used by the Durham quilters.

The major American quilting (as opposed to patchwork) tradition is that of the Amish, the so-called Plain People who

settled in self-sufficient communities first in Pennsylvania in the 18th century and then in the American Midwest. It was, and still is, their practice to use and re-use that which was regarded as essential and to eschew anything that they considered frivolous or unnecessary. Using fabric left over from dressmaking to make quilts was natural, and while highly decorated work was not even considered, pride in their work and perhaps an innate creativity could not be stifled. A number of patterns, probably adapted from their non-Amish neighbors, were gradually adopted as being characteristic of Amish work. The quilts

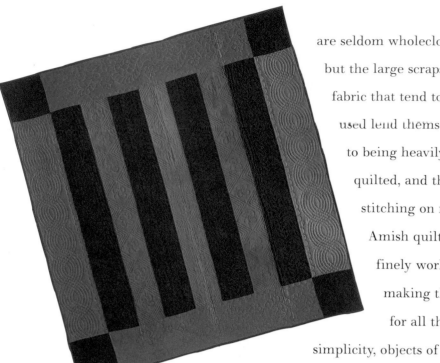

Bars

This lively Amish Bars quilt (c.1920) is certainly related to the somewhat older strippy shown below. The quilting patterns follow each strip with the unusual pumpkin seed design on the blue bars and the stylized bird's wings on the red. The small loops along the inside edge of the border are also out of the ordinary, as is the quilter's use of the wide twisted cable on the vertical sides that changes to feathered cables with flowers interspersed top and bottom.

are seldom wholecloth, but the large scraps of fabric that tend to be used lend themselves to being heavily quilted, and the stitching on most Amish quilts is finely worked, making them, for all their simplicity, objects of great beauty. Amish quilts from the 19th century are highly collectible, and most examples are now in museums or private hands, but the tradition continues, especially in Lancaster County, Pennsylvania, where beautiful quilts made in the old way by Amish quilters can still be purchased.

The patterns used by the Durham quilters and by the Amish have been copied and elaborated upon, and variations of these, and a great many others, abound. Patterns were no doubt exchanged across

Strippy

This lovely strippy, typical of work from the North-east of England, was made in 1899 by Mrs Isabella Calvert for her sister Barbara's marriage. The finely worked quilting follows the strips on the three outside pieces, but the pattern on the center three panels overlaps the edges of the strips most effectively.

the ocean, and the metal or wooden templates used to mark them became treasured family heirlooms. Many of the designs carry regional names, and some were used as symbols, such as the pineapple to represent hospitality or the dove to celebrate a marriage.

QUILTING PATTERNS

The quilt as we know it consists of layers of fabric – usually three – held together by decorative stitching that creates a pattern. The top layer can be a single piece of cloth, known as a wholecloth quilt, or it can be pieced, either as patchwork patterns or from strips of cloth (a "strippy"). The middle layer is made of batting, also known as wadding, a padding originally made from natural fibers such as wool fleece or combed cotton, and now made from the same fibers or from polyester in

Wholecloth

Made in the North-east of England around 1900, this sateen wholecloth quilt is unusual in its lack of the filling patterns which are typical of Durham work, and the use of geometric squared-off borders more often associated with Welsh quilting. The ruffle around three sides is another feature not often found on quilts. The finely worked quilting is very even and precise. The corner fans, in graduated sizes that get smaller nearer the center, are a particularly attractive feature.

various weights or even a blend of polyester and cotton. The bottom layer, called the backing, is generally made from a single piece of plain fabric in a color that coordinates with the top, but fine examples can be found of quilts with a pieced patchwork backing that effectively makes a reversible quilt.

There are many approaches to quilting, and several methods to choose from, but your choices of both technique and pattern will depend on a number of things. Do you want to quilt by hand or machine? Is the quilt top a wholecloth, a strippy or a pieced patchwork pattern? Should the thread be the same color or a contrasting one? What method of marking should you use?

You could choose a design that relates to the pattern of your quilt – for example, echoing curved blocks with curving quilting patterns. However, sometimes curves can be accentuated by quilting judiciously placed straight lines, just as patterns based on straight-sided shapes can be enhanced by quilting worked in sinuous curves. Many patchwork patterns are arranged so that open areas occur between the elements of the design – these are often perfect spaces on which to quilt block or motif patterns.

Simple Grids & Backgrounds

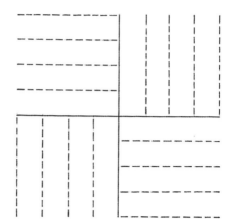

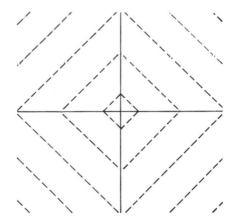

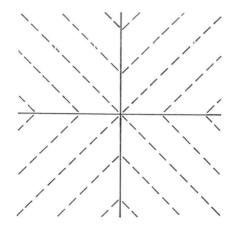

Straight Lines

The simplest of all quilting patterns is of course straight parallel lines. They can be stitched vertically or horizontally, and can cross each other to make a giant grid, or they can be stitched checkerboard fashion, as shown here. The stitches can be large or small, but for best effect they should be even and all the same size.

Diagonal out from the center

Diagonal patterns add movement and vitality to all art forms, and quilting falls into this category. Here, the lines that radiate out from the center in concentric squares are evenly spaced, but the spacing can be varied if you wish. This design works very well on such traditional patterns as Trip Around the World (see page 59).

Diagonal into the center

The center lines cross in the middle and subsequent rows meet along the axis on which they are located. If the entire piece is marked in a grid, this pattern can be combined with the one on the left to give alternating up and down diagonal lines that work very well on simple quilt designs.

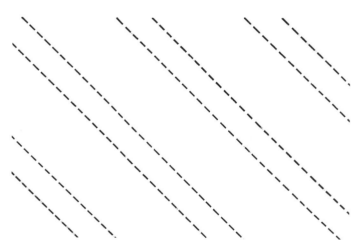

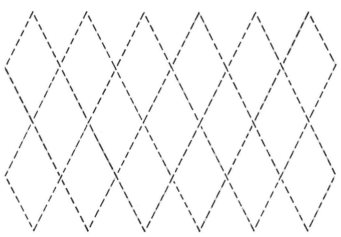

Diagonal

These simple diagonal lines run in one direction only, but lines running on the opposite diagonal could be added and would give a completely different feel to the finished quilt. Single lines in one direction are not as effective as the double lines shown here or triple ones. Remember that accurate marking is essential.

Diamond

Single, evenly spaced diagonal lines running in both directions give a simple but very effective diamond pattern. If double or triple lines are used, the texture of the finished piece becomes even more marked. Diamonds work particularly well on overall square patchwork patterns (see pages 39 and 72–73).

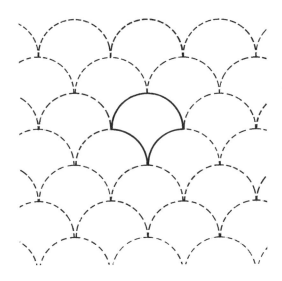

Clamshell

This traditional design is very effective when used with patchwork patterns based on straight lines, or as a background for a medallion or appliquéd quilt. A single basic clamshell shape is outlined in a solid line in the middle of this pattern; this can be traced and enlarged or reduced to fit into the space to be quilted.

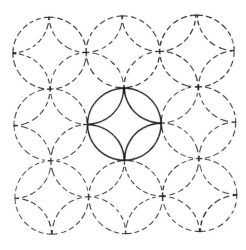

Wineglass

This curved square in a circle can be drawn using a circle of your chosen size. Perhaps wineglasses were used for drafting in the past? It is certainly easy to see the overlaps clearly if the marking is done in this way. The visual reverse of the pattern is a four-petaled flower shape.

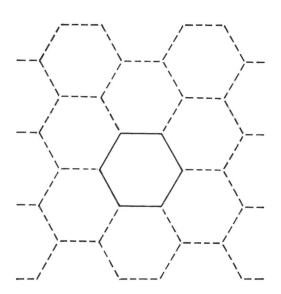

Hexagon

Another traditional design, the basic hexagon shape is very versatile. It works well as an outline or in the ditch with Hexagon patterns (see pages 90–91), and it makes an interesting background for many other designs, both traditional and non-traditional. Trace the solid shape shown and enlarge or reduce it to make a template.

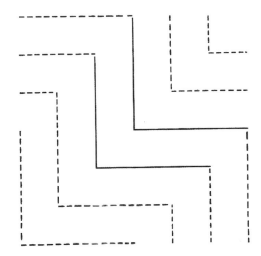

Steps

In this grid pattern, the lines form rectangles that are twice as long as they are wide. Alternated vertically and then horizontally, they create a stepped effect (see Brick, page 42). Careful marking is essential, and although working with a template can be tricky, it is probably easier than drawing the lines with a ruler.

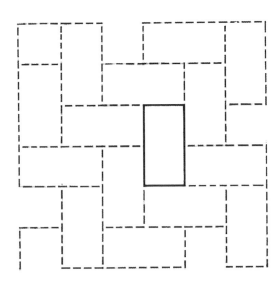

Chevrons

These stepped lines make rectangles that are three times as long as they are wide and create a variation of Steps on the left. If the short edges at the bottom of the vertical shapes and on the right-hand side of the horizontal ones are eliminated, the zigzag pattern is even more clearly defined.

Simple Motifs

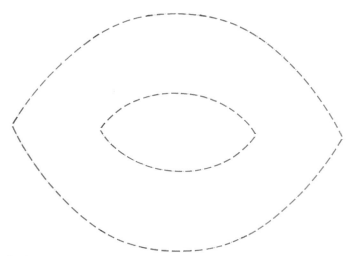

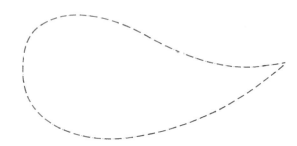

Cable

The cable is one of the most popular of all quilting motifs, and it is renowned for its versatility. Based on a pointed oval, it can be elongated or made more circular. It can be turned into Simple Cable (see opposite) and intricate cables (see page 136) or combined with feathers or diamonds (see pages 136–141).

Feather

Like the cable, the feather is a highly versatile and widely used image for quilting designs. This single frond can be re-drawn, re-sized and combined with others to make Straight Feather (below). It can be made into a flowing cable, a heart or a circle of feathers, or a Feathered Cross or Feathered Swag (see pages 132–133).

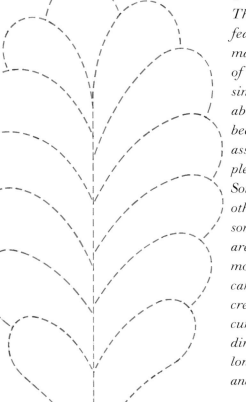

Double Feather

This pattern, like all feather designs, is made up of a number of single feathers, similar to the one above, which have been re-sized and assembled into a pleasing arrangement. Some are bigger than others, some thinner, some overlap. But all are based on the same motif. The elements can be put together to create a feather that curves in either direction or both, or is long and thin or short and wide.

Flower

Flower patterns abound in traditional quilting. This one is traditionally known as a rose, and with the double line as shown, it makes an excellent design for corded quilting (see page 25). In fact, many of the motifs shown in this chapter can be used for corded quilting if the outline is drawn double in this way.

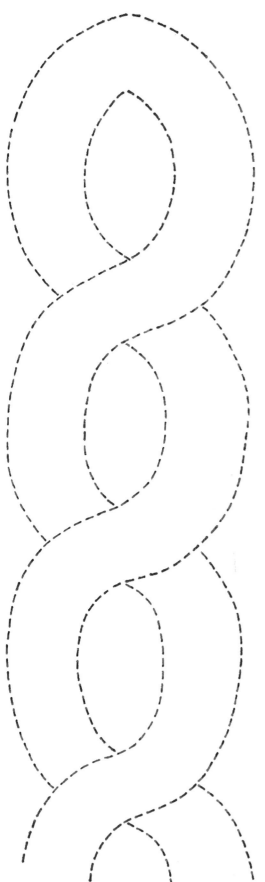

Fan Blade

Another motif that can be used alone or in combination, the Fan Blade here has been given a choice of three tops – straight, curved or pointed. Trace this one or make your own, then cut it out accurately from cardboard or template plastic. Placed side by side, they can be repeated to produce a right-angled, semicircular, or round motif to fill a plain square or circle.

S-curve

This simple motif is really half of a Simple Cable, but it can be drawn easily using an artist's flexible curve (see page 11). Draw one line of the curve, then repeat the same curve a measured distance away from the first. This is another good border or sashing motif, but it is also useful for laying a curved pattern on any quilt. To mark a series of s-curves, make a template and place the top straight edge of the template against the bottom straight edge of the previous curve.

Simple Cable

Cabled patterns of all types are very effective on borders and sashing. Here, the single cable winds down the pattern, overlapping as it goes. To make it longer, simply overlap the open end with the top shown here until the entire border has been marked. You can make the template longer in the same way, but this is not necessary; just keep moving the template down until you reach the bottom. To finish, turn the template upside down and draw around the rounded end.

Blocks

Heart

The familiar heart shape has been used in patterns for as long as design has been known. It is simple and straightforward, and capable of enormous variation. To use it for corded quilting (see page 25), simply draw a second line ¹/4 in (5 mm) inside or outside the shape.

Fleur-de-lis

The traditional fleur-de-lis pattern appears in many forms on quilts from all eras. Here, it consists of a simple outline that is easy to stitch, but it can be made more complex by making four copies and placing the bases together to make a square shape, as in Four Hearts.

Four Hearts

This more complicated heart pattern makes a beautiful filling for a plain block. It can be enlarged to fill the surface of a cushion cover. If the top indentations of the heart shapes are rounded off, a four-leaf clover shape can be created.

Tulip Ring

Tulips are another motif widely used on quilts, especially appliquéd work. Their pleasing shape is simple to quilt, and the ring shown here is a good pattern to use for filling a plain block or making a quilted cushion. An individual tulip shape can easily be turned into a design for corded quilting or trapunto (see page 25).

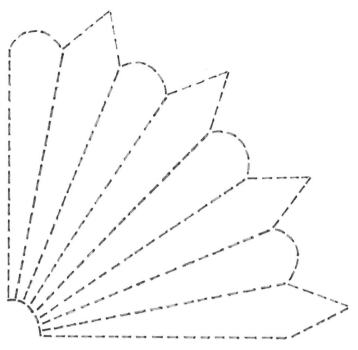

Square Swirl

This design, based on a simple feather shape (see page 125), is ideal for filling a plain square shape, or it could be used to make an overall quilting pattern for a patchwork quilt. If each line is doubled, it makes an interesting motif for corded quilting (see page 25). Its potential is limitless — it can be made more intricate with more blades, while the corner shapes can be made larger or smaller.

Fan

The fan block pattern can be used with Grandmother's Fan (see page 108), or it can fill the corner of a plain square. The tops of the fan blades can be rounded, pointed or straight, or alternated as shown here. Combining four fan shapes along the straight edges creates a traditional plate design (see page 109).

Shell

There are endless designs taken from nature, and the variations on shell patterns are equally infinite. This form, probably based on a nautilus shell, looks intricate but is actually quite straightforward to stitch — just take care to keep the spiral evenly spaced. Shell patterns are useful for filling irregular shapes or for creating texture on patchwork quilts, especially ones with a nautical theme.

Clamshell

This shell variation goes well into a plain circle or square. Its elegant design would look good as a cushion cover — try it scattered around in various sizes. It can, of course, be enlarged or reduced, and the spacing and placement of the curved edges can be altered.

Exploding Star

Stars rank high on the list of traditional and widely used patterns for quilting as well as patchwork. This five-pointed version begins with a small star in the center outlined with larger, but otherwise identical, ones. You could, of course, continue expanding the star until you reach the edges of the quilt or cushion.

Five-pointed Star

Here, the star is fashioned as five irregular diamonds which meet in the center and are then outlined on the inside of each individual shape. It works well on a star-studded quilt, or as a motif in a plain square or circle.

Oak Leaf and Reel

This traditional twelve-pointed star is based on a double hexagon and can be used to great effect in plain square or circular patches. It can be altered in any number of ways — try making the outer points longer or eliminating the central circle.

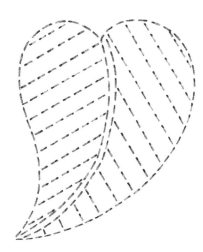

Grape Leaf

This traditional broken leaf consists of an s-shaped central stem with thin leaves that are graduated in size along it. It has many possibilities, in both its variety and its uses. The stem, for instance, could be corded and the leaves stuffed as trapunto (see page 25) to make an interesting and unusual wholecloth pattern.

Leaf

This simple shape has been embellished with parallel lines of quilting from the outside edges to the central stem, giving a feeling of movement to an otherwise static image. The curving outline without the straight lines could easily be adapted for corded quilting.

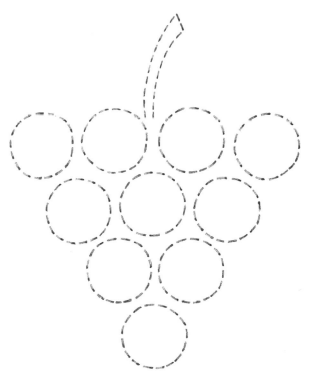

Grapes

This cluster of fruit, another example of a natural motif adapted for design, is a good pattern to use for trapunto work (see page 25), as well as a simple block pattern for quilting. Try combining it with a Grape Leaf or two from above right.

Tulip

The ever-popular Tulip makes a stunning single motif for a plain block, and it also works well as a design for corded quilting (see page 25). Simply double the outlines, $1/4$ in (5 mm) apart, or eliminate all but the outside outlines first.

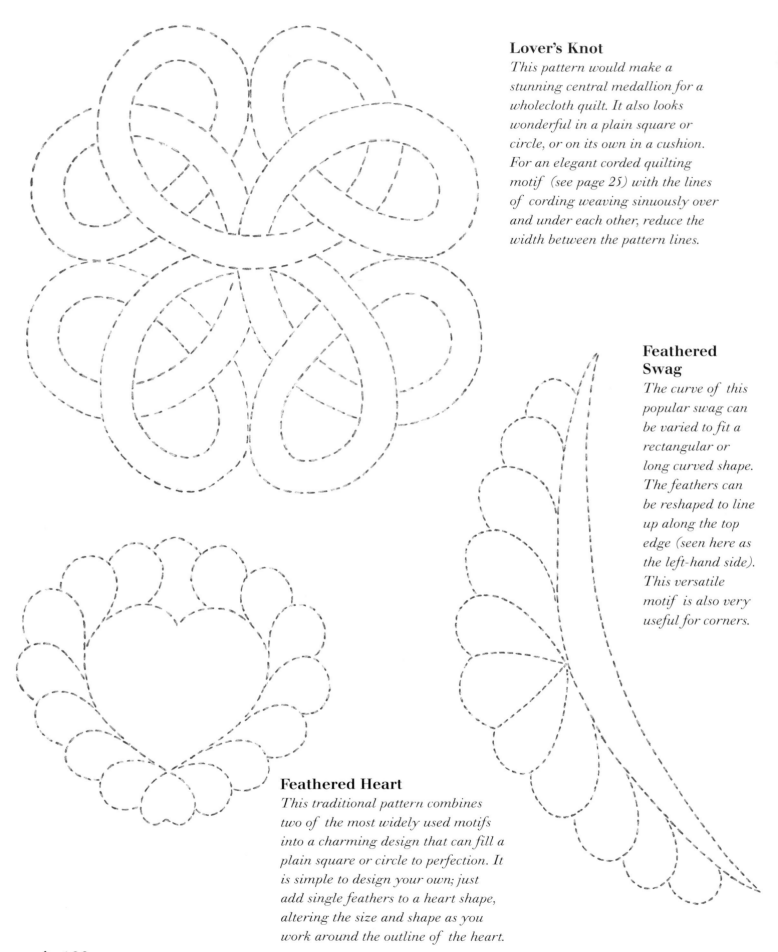

Lover's Knot

This pattern would make a stunning central medallion for a wholecloth quilt. It also looks wonderful in a plain square or circle, or on its own in a cushion. For an elegant corded quilting motif (see page 25) with the lines of cording weaving sinuously over and under each other, reduce the width between the pattern lines.

Feathered Swag

The curve of this popular swag can be varied to fit a rectangular or long curved shape. The feathers can be reshaped to line up along the top edge (seen here as the left-hand side). This versatile motif is also very useful for corners.

Feathered Heart

This traditional pattern combines two of the most widely used motifs into a charming design that can fill a plain square or circle to perfection. It is simple to design your own; just add single feathers to a heart shape, altering the size and shape as you work around the outline of the heart.

Feathered Cross

This cross-shaped motif is often seen filling the plain blocks on Irish Chain quilts (see page 46), but it is obviously far more versatile than that. It can be made longer or shorter, thinner or wider, and the shape of the cross can be altered as the space to be quilted dictates. As with all the block motifs in this section, it is tailor-made to enhance plain areas on a patchwork piece, but can be adapted to suit many other situations, from cushion covers to a more overall effect on simple quilts.

Feathered Circle

These two pages show the adaptability of the simple feather motif quite clearly. Virtually any line you can draw can be enhanced with feathers, and this circle is no exception. It can, of course, be made larger or smaller, but in addition the size and shape of the feathers can be changed to suit other elements in an overall design.

Straight Borders

Interlocked Squares

Border patterns can, of course, be used in places other than borders. They can run along sashing strips or be stitched as the motif in one section of a strippy quilt. The square, an ever-useful friend, is here turned on point and interlocked with its partner on either side to make a diamond-patterned border. The depth of the crossovers can be altered — the small squares can be made tiny or the corner of one can touch the corner of the next square down. To extend the pattern, simply line up the top of the template or stencil with the bottom of the pattern that you have already traced.

Double Interlocked Squares

This pattern is a variation of the one on the left, with parallel lines drawn inside each square. By threading the interlocked lines under and over each other, you can create a very attractive chain effect. The same technique can be used with circular or oval shapes. Draw several interlocking shapes to see if you like the look.

Interlocked Hexagons

These coffin-shaped hexagons interlock in the same way as the square patterns on the left, but the crossover here creates a square on point that divides automatically into four sections. If one of the intersecting lines is eliminated, the chain link is reinforced, while the interlocking disappears entirely if the square is left blank. Try it on a tracing to see if you like the effect.

Diamond Twist

A doubled straight line that bends at just over 90 degrees each time it hits the side of its imaginary channel creates a wide diamond pattern. The chain is fluid and sinuous, without a curved line in sight. As with all such border stencils, the pattern can be extended by lapping the top end of the template over the bottom end of the marked pattern to line it up.

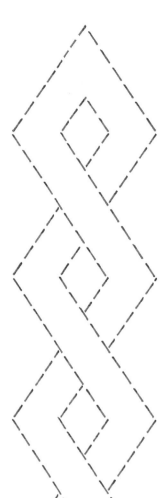

Diamond Border

In this diamond border, the lines intersect in both directions to create a series of contiguous small diamonds inside pointed peaks and troughs. Because the angle is steeper than in Diamond Twist above, the look is much more angular.

Curved Borders

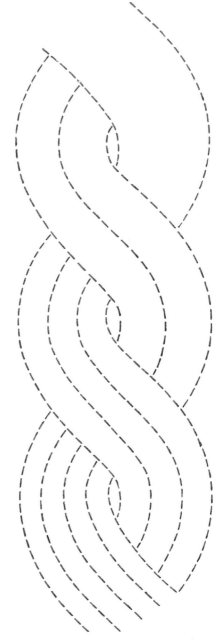

Cable

The simple cable consists of curved parallel lines that weave their way over and under each other. The pattern can be varied in the width of the cable itself, and by adding lines between the cable lines – here, we show sections with one, two and three central lines. As with the straight border templates, the pattern is extended by overlapping top and bottom to line up the next section, but make sure the stencil is straight in the section being marked.

Braided Cable

The pattern above is made up of two ropes, but here three ropes are plaited together to create a more intricate cable that can also be altered by adding lines within the channels.

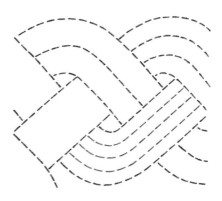

Feathered Twist

One of the most popular of all cable patterns, this twist combines a simple cable with a continuous Running Feather. The cable is the basis of the design, and the size of the central oval determines the width of the pattern and the size of the feathers.

Tulips

This pretty pattern can be extended by lining up the bottom stem with the bit of stem shown at the top of the template. The stems can be lengthened to give more space between the flowers, and the leaves can be altered or eliminated. An effective variation could be made by substituting a rose, or another floral or leaf shape for the tulip.

Pumpkin Seed

Legend has it that this pattern is named after the seed that was used as its template. It is an adaptable pattern widely seen on Amish quilts, and can be accomplished surprisingly easily on the machine, since the seeds are constructed as figures of eight, and the lines that enclose them can be worked up one side and down the other. As with Tulips (left), a portion of a seed is shown at the top of the template to make it easy to line up the pattern when you are marking the quilt.

Diamond Cable

This elegant pattern combines the cable from the opposite page with the Diamond Twist on page 135. Equally effective without the center line, the border can be made even more complex by altering the size and shape of the ovals and squares.

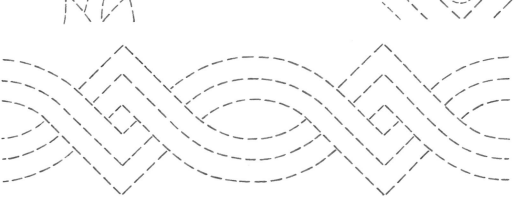

Corners

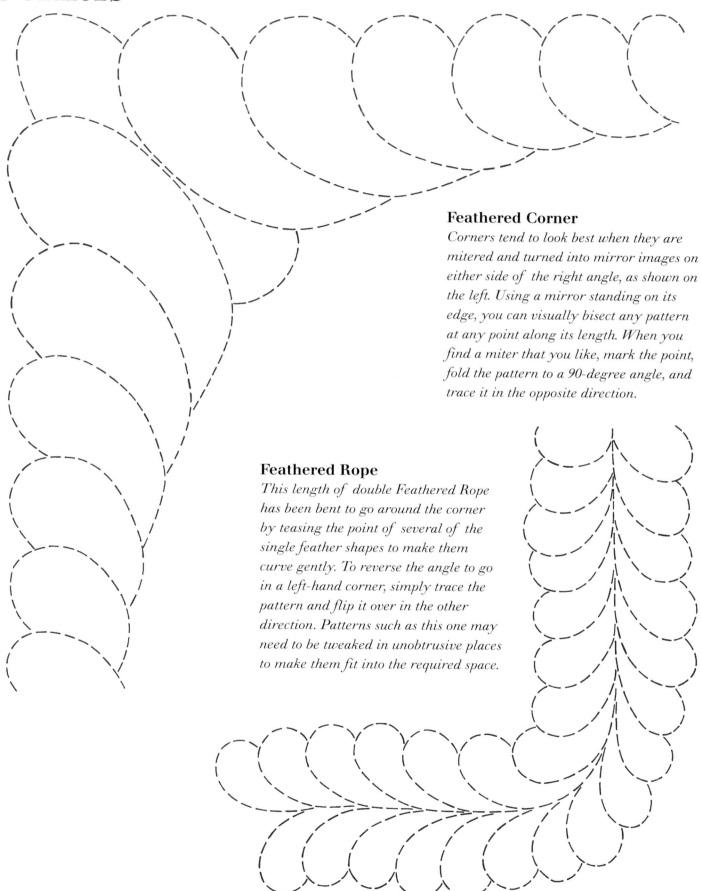

Feathered Corner

Corners tend to look best when they are mitered and turned into mirror images on either side of the right angle, as shown on the left. Using a mirror standing on its edge, you can visually bisect any pattern at any point along its length. When you find a miter that you like, mark the point, fold the pattern to a 90-degree angle, and trace it in the opposite direction.

Feathered Rope

This length of double Feathered Rope has been bent to go around the corner by teasing the point of several of the single feather shapes to make them curve gently. To reverse the angle to go in a left-hand corner, simply trace the pattern and flip it over in the other direction. Patterns such as this one may need to be tweaked in unobtrusive places to make them fit into the required space.

Pumpkin Seed

The Pumpkin Seed border (see page 137) is easy to turn. Simply finish the horizontal row and line the pattern up vertically to continue down the side. Reverse the direction when you reach the bottom right-hand corner, then reverse again at bottom left, and so on. This border will look best if the pumpkin-seed motif appears in the center of the top and bottom and continues as shown. If you begin by drawing the correct number of squares on point to fill the edge, it should be straightforward to fill in the pumpkin seeds to the appropriate size.

Simple Twist

There are myriad ways of taking a cable pattern around a corner. For this elegant solution, the edge of the final loop has been bisected and joined with a narrow gap between the ovals at each end. With all border patterns, it is possible to finish the motif at the edge of the quilt without turning, or to leave the corner space blank and fill it with a separate block motif, but rounding the corner provides a continuity that is usually desirable.

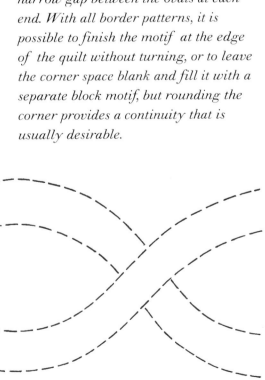

Leaf and Vine

This dainty traditional pattern consists of two sinuously curving parallel lines that round the corner in a deep bend, which gives room to place a leaf or two in its center. The number of leaves can be altered, as can the distance between them, and the curves of the line can be made deeper or shallower.

Arc

Also known as Shell or Fan, this pattern is most appropriate as a corner on its own, perhaps on a wide border with simple vertical and horizontal stitching. It can also be effective in plain setting blocks and looks especially appropriate used to fill the empty corner of a Fan block (page 108). The section in the corner itself is based on a quarter-circle, while the other motifs are parts of a half-circle.

Cable Twist

Here, the two strands of the cable diverge at the corner to keep the flow of the pattern, with the under-and-over effect elegantly maintained. One goes up into a steep curve to round the corner, while the other flattens out to slide under it. Line up the straight part of the pattern to extend it in either direction, and reverse the pattern to make the corner bend the opposite way. See pages 127–128 and 136 for more information on cable designs.

Diamond Cable

This is the simplest version of the Diamond Cable border on page 137, showing the easiest way to turn the corner with it. It consists of two arching outlines that cross each other to make the ovals and the diamonds. Here, the corner is formed by joining the ends of the inside arc in a point and simply rounding off the outside arcs to pass through the resulting thin oval shape.

Index

Acknowledgements

Author's Acknowledgements

With thanks to David, Daniel and Joshua.

And to the following people who contributed so much:
Ann Israel and Rebecca Arscott for their stitching. Valerie Atkins and Yvette Barton, and the staff at Creative Quilting, 3 Bridge Road, Hampton Court, Surrey KT8 9EU. Catherine Ward for the editing. Matthew Ward and Sampson Lloyd for the photographs. Kate Simunek and David Ashby for the illustrations. Sarah Hoggett, Julia Ward-Hastelow, Tiffany Jenkins, Corinne Asghar and Katie Bent.

Picture Credits

page 1: Beamish, The North of England Open Air Museum;
pages 2–3: America Hurrah Archive, NYC; pages 6–7: The American Museum in Britain; pages 28–29: America Hurrah Archive, NYC; page 30: York Museum; page 31: The American Museum in Britain; page 32: America Hurrah Archive, NYC; 33: America Hurrah Archive, NYC (both); pages 50–51: Maggi McCormick Gordon; page 52: America Hurrah Archive, NYC; page 53: The American Museum in Britain; page 54: Beamish, The North of England Open Air Museum; page 55: Maggi McCormick Gordon (top); Beamish, The North of England Open Air Museum (bottom); pages 84–85: Beamish, The North of England Open Air Museum; page 86: York Museum; page 87: Beamish, The North of England Open Air Museum; page 88: The American Museum in Britain; page 89: The American Museum in Britain; pages 100–101: America Hurrah Archive, NYC; page 102: The American Museum in Bath; page 103: America Hurrah Archive, NYC (both); page 104: America Hurrah Archive, NYC; page 105: The American Museum in Britain; pages 118–119: Beamish, The North of England Open Air Museum; page 120: America Hurrah Archive, NYC; page 121: Beamish, The North of England Open Air Museum; page 122: America Hurrah Archive, NYC (top); Beamish, The North of England Open Air Museum (bottom); page 123: Beamish, The North of England Open Air Museum.